URBAN WARRIOR

URBAN WARRIOR

MY DEADLY LIFE WITH THE POLICE ARMED RESPONSE UNIT

HELEN BARNETT
WITH
HELEN ARMITAGE

BLAKE

Published by Blake Publishing Ltd,
3 Bramber Court, 2 Bramber Road,
London W14 9PB, England

First published in 1999

ISBN 1 85782 322 X

British Library Cataloguing-in-Publication Data:
A catalogue record for this book is available
from the British Library.

Design: GDAdesign

Printed in Great Britain by
Creative Print and Design (Wales), Ebbw Vale, Gwent

1 3 5 7 9 10 8 6 4 2

Every effort has been made to contact the relevant copyright-holders, but some were
unobtainable. We would be grateful if the appropriate owners would contact us.

CONTENTS

ACKNOWLEDGEMENTS   xi

A POEM FOR HELEN   xiii

CHAPTER ONE

THE SHOOTING: BOXING DAY 1994   15

CHAPTER TWO

THE MAKING OF A POLICE CADET   25

CHAPTER THREE

BIG CITY BEAT   53

CHAPTER FOUR

MARRIAGE, MOTHERHOOD
AND NOT HAVING IT ALL   79

CHAPTER FIVE

THE STABBING: CARELESS
IN THE COMMUNITY   101

CHAPTER SIX

DISTRESS, BULIMIA AND DIVORCE   135

CHAPTER SEVEN

THE BOMBING: AN IRA DOUBLE   159

CHAPTER EIGHT

CLIMBING THE RANKS AND FALLING APART   181

CHAPTER NINE

ONCE IS AN ACCIDENT, TWICE IS UNLUCKY, THREE TIMES... MY THIRD BRUSH WITH DEATH   199

CHAPTER TEN

THE HEARTBREAK: ENOUGH IS ENOUGH   231

CHAPTER ELEVEN

STARTING OVER   249

To Ben

ACKNOWLEDGEMENTS

To Roger Gray, whose idea it first was for this book; to
Robert Kirby, who was prescient enough to take it on and
persistent enough to pursue it; to Helen Armitage, who
listened so well and took my words and turned them into
something; to John Blake for taking a punt; to Hazel Orme
for an excellent edit and Adam Parfitt for his co-operation
and unflappability; to CJ and Marion, whose friendship
I value most specially; to Barry, John and Jeni Law,
formerly Lawson, who so generously shared their memories
with me; to my parents, my brother, my children, and to
Steve, without whose love, support and baby-sitting,
none of this would have been so easy.
Thank you all in different ways.

A POEM FOR HELEN

I've cried the tears of a hero,
With my ways I've been a prisoner,
I felt the pain of a saint,
And, the glory of being a winner.

I no longer need comfort,
For it's comfort I now give,
I understand my pain,
So that I can now live.

You will never know my hurt,
Or experience my pain,
I'm working for a new life,
So it will never happen again.

I'll show you my true colours,
No longer in black and white,
I'm as bright as any star,
I can blind you with my light.

I don't fear the unknown,
Just as a child at birth,
So give me a firm place to stand,
For I can move the earth.

My tears expose my inner self,
Just like an open book,
It isn't hard to see me,
Just take a deeper look.

CJ
FOR YOUR WEDDING,
27 SEPTEMBER 1997

CHAPTER 1

THE SHOOTING: BOXING DAY 1994

By 6.30 a.m. Boxing Day I was on duty at Old Street, one of three crew for Armed Response Vehicle Trojan 521. At the start of my shift I had booked out two weapons from the armoury — my Glock personal issue 9mm self-loading pistol, and a Heckler & Koch MP5 carbine. I also signed out four magazines, two for my Glock, two for my MP5. I loaded my Glock and put it in the holster I'd strapped to my body; the MP5 I secured in the safe of our car. As a member of Scotland Yard's firearms squad, SO19, this was all part and parcel of our routine daily patrol of north London.

We were early turn, just about to finish. It was shortly before two in the afternoon. We'd gone back to base at Old Street, near the City, when the call came in that they needed some firearms units up in Enfield, north London. So off we went, even though it was minutes from the end of our shift.

It had been a long couple of days. To make the six o'clock start on Boxing Day I'd driven up to London from my parents' home in Worcestershire on Christmas night, leaving Ben, my four-year-old, with his grandparents. We'd spent a relaxed Christmas together, and it had been a wrench to leave them, especially Ben and especially at that time of year. He'd been so excited about it all, and I really wanted to spend the time with him. As usual I was torn, but as usual the job had to come first.

It was 1.45 p.m. when we received the call requesting we make our way to Ponders End police station in Enfield to liaise with other Armed Response Vehicles (ARVs). We left Old Street immediately and reached Ponders End station around two. Some of our colleagues were already there, being briefed by an inspector and the local duty officer about a siege in Enfield, in which a sixteen-month-old toddler had been taken hostage by her father.

Alan McMinn had abducted his baby daughter in the climax to a domestic that had been going on over Christmas. His relationship with Sarah Miles, his estranged partner, had erupted into violence on Christmas Eve. She had gone to the police then, when he allegedly kicked her in the face and fractured her nose. Finally, in a fit of fury and frustration on Boxing Day, he'd snatched their daughter, Georgia.

Miles had seen a gun concealed in the front of his trousers, tucked into his belt. Alan McMinn had had access to guns previously but on this occasion, with their child involved, she had decided to call the police. On the drive to Enfield it crossed my mind briefly that while Ben was opening his presents on Christmas morning, while we were sitting round the table enjoying the turkey and trimmings, while we were cocooned in the warmth of the festive season, the McMinns had been out in the cold. Their Christmas had taken on the dimensions of nightmare.

The description we were given of McMinn was quite basic but nevertheless distinctive — white male, dark-haired, thirtyish, probably wearing a sheepskin coat, and almost certainly in possession of a gun and a young child in a pushchair. There was a final twist to the tale. McMinn was already wanted by the police for armed robbery as well as for questioning about attempted murder. Whichever way you looked at it, it was bad news: a violent criminal holding hostage an innocent child had all the elements of real-life tragedy.

Among the firearms teams at the siege was specialist firearms officer PC Nick Tinning, who was part of the next level up from the ARV unit to which I belonged. Nick had considerably more experience than me. I was asked to accompany him to do a recce of McMinn's address at 30A Ordnance Road, Enfield. Our brief was to provide a rough sketch of the flat, its access and its location. This would assist us in the event of an armed siege, if McMinn refused to surrender himself peacefully.

Nick and I borrowed civilian jackets to carry out our recce in as low-key a way as possible. Over my uniform I put on a multicoloured padded jacket, warm enough for a cold winter's day but more suited to a race down some sparkling white Swiss ski slope than an armed police mission on the grey streets of north London. We left Ponders End station, and drove swiftly in an unmarked police car to Ordnance Road.

With most people relaxing at home over the Christmas period, the streets weren't exactly busy that winter afternoon, so there was every chance that McMinn might have stayed indoors. What we didn't know was that he and baby Georgia were, in fact, inside the flat. McMinn had barricaded them both in, along with an arsenal of knives. He'd actually watched us as we approached the front door. Fortunately he'd not taken advantage of his cover to strike out. In any case we were to meet up with him sooner rather than later.

Rejoining our colleagues, we began to form into a considerable siege combat force on the streets of Enfield. Suddenly, from nowhere, I felt extremely tired. We'd had an early start, and I was ready to go home. But I couldn't give in to it. I had to be stronger than that. Any thoughts of a cosy family Christmas had to be firmly expelled from my mind.

I lived and breathed my job. It was as far from a cosy

nine-to-five as I was at that moment from a hot bath, a hot dinner and four-year-old Ben, who was spending another Christmas without me. I was twenty-eight years old. I'd been married and was now separated. But in fact I was still married — to the job. I'd been in the police service for ten years, and I'd never known when my work ended and my home life began. What a luxury that would be! One that none of us could afford. The service was my life. A life in service. That was what we'd had drummed into us at Hendon police college. Don't get me wrong. I loved it. But did it love me?

A full contingent of ARVs and support vehicles had turned up. Standing by on the pavement Nick and I were discussing strategy. Out of the corner of my eye I noticed officers putting on their body armour. Before we could do anything sensible like that, there was a sudden squeal of brakes as another police vehicle turned up, followed immediately by a shout: 'That's him!'

A few yards away from where I stood I saw him, clad in the sheepskin coat and wheeling the young child in a push-chair. This was to be my first and only encounter with Alan McMinn — apart from the subsequent, distressing sightings of him during his trial. He was trying to propel the baby buggy away from him and into the road. Next to me Nick leapt into action and started to run forward, attempting to reach McMinn and push the pram out of the way for a clear run at him.

In the middle of the road McMinn hesitated momentarily before he spun sharply on his heels. Facing me directly now, he began to walk backwards into the centre of the junction. As he did so he drew a small black handgun from inside his sheepskin coat and shouted defiantly, 'Yeah, it's me!'

I ran towards him and pulled my Glock from its holster. I remember feeling incredibly frightened and began to operate on automatic pilot, my extensive training kicking in to help me. This was real and happening to me now. It was no rehearsal.

I felt shocked by the volume of aggression that McMinn had turned on us. He was armed, and I feared he might lose his cool, snap and start shooting at random. God knows what might happen then. Yards away people were waiting at a bus stop. Most worrying was that McMinn might decide to use his child as a human shield.

Instead he did something surprising and turned his gun on himself. Using both his hands he put the barrel in his mouth. His knuckles were locked white on the butt of that weapon. It was a brief though dramatic gesture that was followed immediately by a glint of metal as he changed his mind and yanked the pistol from his mouth. Now he pointed it straight at me.

I was level with the rear bumper of a police car parked on the road junction, my right leg to the fore, when he pulled the trigger. It all happened in the blink of an eye. There was a plume of smoke and an ear-shattering blast; I felt like I'd been hit on the knee with a sledgehammer. It was as if it weren't happening to me. Nothing had prepared me for this.

At first I felt detached and experienced no pain. I was aware only of people shouting, of a swell of men's voices yelling a variety of instructions, urgently, disjointedly, all at once: 'Armed police!' 'Put the gun down!' It was all over in a matter of seconds. But the long and the short of it was that I'd been hit on my leg with a force equal to a four-ton weight dropping from a great height. That's the impact of a bullet when it meets a human target, the way it crashes through flesh and bone, nerves and muscles. I dropped to my left knee at the bumper of the adjacent car, covering McMinn all the while with my gun.

It was all hazy from then on, to say the least. I must have been in shock. All my senses were dulled, and I can't remember hearing any more bangs, or anything else at all. Suddenly the incident had descended into a frenzy of violence that erupted as if from nowhere like a huge black cloud to block out the sun. Everything just stopped, and I was conscious only of the immense danger ahead of me. For the first time I thought about my own safety as I slowly edged towards the cover of the police vehicle.

I lay on the ground behind the car, no longer anaesthetised by shock or the rush of adrenaline that goes with it. Nothing mattered except the extreme pain in my leg. When I felt it was safe I put my gun down beside me and nursed my wounded knee. The pain became more acute. I didn't dare look at my leg. Instead I turned away and saw McMinn prostrate in a pool of blood on the footway, a couple of officers by his side. After I'd been shot, the others had opened fire and shot him five times in the arm, leg and abdomen.

McMinn was later rushed to hospital by air ambulance, as baby Georgia was reunited with her mum. I can only imagine how Georgia's mum must have felt, waiting for news of her child. And the terror that child must have experienced, trapped in the middle of a raging gun battle. It's the kind of thing that scars you for life. For his part McMinn got off relatively unscathed, considering, and survived his serious injuries; in the papers the day after the shooting, it was reported that I was recovering from mine — also serious but not life-threatening. Indeed, the damage was not a risk to my physical survival, but it was to threaten me later in other, less obvious but more insidious ways.

I began to glance nervously around me. All the people in the bus queue had gone, had evaporated into thin air, no doubt hiding, terrified, in doorways or behind parked cars. As I looked across the road I was glad to see the familiar face of PS Richard Gladman. We had been PCs together at Hornsey, and Richard was now a sergeant at Enfield. From behind the police car where he was crouched, I heard him shout, 'Somebody's down. One of yours has been hit.' We made eye contact across the road. 'Someone's down,' he said again, shouting louder as he looked straight at me, reassuringly.

When it was safe to break cover he came over to where I lay. I had an overwhelming sense of *déjà vu*. I'd been here before. At first Richard could only stare down at me in horror. I could see the shock written all over his face, his outrage at what had happened to me. Not to me. Not again. I remember saying to him, 'Not again, Richard. Not again. Why me? Not again!' I had tears in my eyes as I just kept on repeating myself.

Within moments other officers appeared at my side to help and encourage me. Tony Hall, a colleague in the Firearms Unit, started cutting up the navy blue worsted of my blood-soaked trouser leg to get to the wound and do some basic first aid on the considerable damage a .38 bullet can do to the human body.

Fortunately, an ambulance that was already in attendance — standard police procedure during any call-out to a firearms incident — got to me quickly. The crew took off my jacket, unclipped my belt rig to remove my gun and put a drip in my arm. As they were doing this I heard the familiar, ominous sound of the whirring blades of the medical helicopter. It sent shivers up my spine as I remembered the last time.

A posse of my colleagues stood above me in a protective circle, appalled to a man by my plight. It had happened to me, though it might have happened to any of them. All in a day's police work, an indisputable hazard of belonging to one of the most dangerous units in the Metropolitan Police Force, but once more I was the one who'd been hurt in the line of duty. One of only a handful of women, and the only mother, in a unit of several hundred men.

One by one even the toughest and most hard-bitten of my colleagues squatted down beside me to hold my hand and say, 'You'll be OK, Helen. You'll be OK.' This time, though, I wasn't so sure.

CHAPTER 2

THE MAKING OF A POLICE CADET

Not me! It's something I've thought all my life. I've never really believed in myself. Whenever I won anything, from sports' prizes at school right through to the Baton of Honour when I left Hendon Police Training School, I always thought, It can't possibly be me. Even when I talk about it now it all seems oddly disconnected; I still find it hard to credit. Just like when I see myself in back copies of the *Daily Mail* or the *Telegraph*, I find it impossible to reconcile the headlines 'Heroine PC' or 'Crackshot Policewoman' with me, let alone 'Britain's Bravest Policewoman', the description they once gave of me in the *Express*.

For all the years I was growing up in the small village of Childswickham in the Vale of Evesham, not a lot happened. It had once been a busier place. The old Roman road that went from London to Worcester passed right through its centre, and from 1763 it was the main coaching road to London. The Celtic origins of the name are Clearing in the Wood in the Vale, and the village was owned by the monastery in Evesham. We lived five miles from what is now the small market town of Evesham, still famous for what remains of its abbey as well as its 110-foot-high bell tower. Childswickham is set in the prettiest countryside, a mile and a half from picturesque Broadway, famous for the crowning beauty of its main street, where houses of honey-coloured Cotswold stone stand back across broad green verges. This was English rural life at its best — and its quietest.

In our village a brook runs by the roadside that leads to a Norman church and a seventeenth-century inn. A slender cross sets the scene for the tower and spire of the church, backed by the long line of the Cotswold Hills. In the churchyard lies Mary Lane, who died when she was 133. This is the kind of place you don't want to leave, and, when I was raised there in the sixties and seventies, there was no imperative to do so. With the village shop and primary school, the pub and the church, it was all so self-contained. And so were we.

Mine was an uneventful childhood. Fish and chips were a real treat. There was no McDonald's and not much money about. Cheltenham, home of National Hunt racing, the Ladies' College and the epitome of English gentility, is fifteen miles away. From time to time we'd go shopping there for clothes. But, largely, we made our own fun, usually outdoors, playing by the brook across the fields for hours, jumping over it, occasionally falling in. We'd go exploring in the woods. We were always outside in our jeans and wellingtons, getting muddy. I was a child who liked the fresh air, was physically active, not at all bookish. When I was eight I got my first pony, Jinni, who was a bit of a handful: her main aim was to get me out of the saddle, and the overhanging branches of the apple trees in the orchard were her secret weapon. But her determination to knock me off was equal to mine to stay on. Stalemate. It's often been like that for me. I know I'm a very determined person, once I set my mind on something. One of my great-grandfathers was still following the local hunt on foot when he was ninety. I think determination runs in the family.

My family have lived in this picture book part of England for generations. My father took over the market-gardening business from his father, who in turn inherited it from my great-grandfather. My father's father, my grandfather, died when my dad was fourteen, so it was a big responsibility on his shoulders at an early age. Dad worked with his brother, seven days a week when we were kids — both of my parents did. They had a market stall in Banbury, stocked with fruit from the orchards they owned as well as vegetables they grew on a sizeable acreage of plots in and around the village. At one stage, when we were young and the business was thriving, they had three or four women to help them cultivate the crops: cabbage, lettuce and peppers, parsley, beans and celery. Dad retired just recently, but there was no one in the family to take over the business. In any case, market-gardening is a dying art. All those family-run traditional garden-produce businesses in the Vale of Evesham are becoming extinct, much like the corner shop, overtaken by the vast scale of the supermarkets and huge quantities that are now imported. There's no money in it, just a lot of hard work for little reward.

Until I left home to join the Metropolitan Police Cadet Corps when I was eighteen, all I recall is how my parents worked all the time. They were immensely diligent, as much by choice as necessity; the nature of the business required it. Fortunately, Gran, my maternal grandmother, lived nearby, as near to us as was possible without living with us: in a caravan at the bottom of our garden. It was fully kitted out; she even had her own TV. She'd moved there a year after she was widowed in 1966, the year I was born, and became a vital part of the big extended family in which I grew up. I was very fond of her, and she was really good to us. We had a ritual that I'll never forget. Every night before I went to sleep I'd bang on my bedroom window and wait for her to pull back the curtain of her caravan and wave me goodnight.

It was like that there then. People looked out for one another, cared about each other; in the village itself, with a population that even now numbers no more than seven hundred, we all knew our neighbours, even just enough to say hello; there was a wonderful spirit of community. The local bobby was part of that, too, respected in the area and involved in all sorts of things, not just turning up at the scene of a crime. It was a profession that was far more respected then, especially in rural Britain. The police were the ones who sorted things out, part of the glue that held us all together. This appealed to me, especially as I got older, fitted my personality. I liked the idea of helping people, though in hindsight I consider this view of the role of the police as naïve. Certainly, as I was to discover, the reality of life for a serving officer in London was very different. As a child in an idyllic rural community with a stable family background, I didn't know how lucky I was. Now that I have seen some of the horrors of domestic life, I realise this even more. In the course of my police work I was to meet types of people I didn't know even existed at the time. London was to come as a huge shock, but you soon learn to adapt; some things, though, I never got used to.

I'd become interested in horses, and they remained an obsession for years. As my parents weren't especially well-off, it must have been something of a sacrifice for them to buy me my own pony, which is what they did when I joined the North Cotswold Hunt, and I achieved Pony Club Efficiency Certificates, Standard C and D. I also had the first of what proved a series of increasingly ominous lessons about life — albeit on this occasion not life-threatening — when out riding with a friend one August at haymaking time. I heard the combine harvester coming from a way off, and so did my pony, but it didn't stop her being spooked as it drew near and leaving me in a ditch with a broken leg. It was the end of the summer holidays, and I was about to start at middle school, Bredon Hill. I did so with my leg in plaster up to my thigh. But I didn't let it slow me down. I even remember climbing a hill to go kite flying. A broken leg didn't stop me. Mum had to take me back to Worcester Hospital to get the cast repaired because I'd been so active that I'd worn it down at the foot. I've always been like that. If you live, you expect knocks. If you stay indoors, it's safe enough, but there's not much living in it. If you venture out into the world things happen, good and bad. It's all part of life. But I had to learn to temper this attitude eventually, when it wasn't so much about life as death.

It was at Bredon Hill that I began to get involved in team sports. I guess I've always been a team player. As a child I was sociable, and at school I was popular. I liked to fit in and take part. At Bredon Hill a friend and I were chosen to make the teachers tea and coffee at break-time. It was a privilege to be asked to do this, however ingratiating it may sound now, and we really enjoyed our responsibilities. It made me feel important. On the whole I was an obedient child, but at home I could be short-tempered and irritable. I always gave myself to everything I did, and that took up a lot of energy. I'm still like that. Something has to give, and those closest to me suffer as a consequence. When I was subsequently awarded the school prize for achievement in sport, though, I remember feeling over the moon.

Looking back to the team sports at school, I enjoyed hockey and athletics in particular. I'd never miss a practice session and moved heaven and earth to make sure I got there. I was Worcestershire champion at shot-put and javelin when I was twelve, and won the Amateur Athletic Association Three, Four and Five Star Awards in my early teens; representing South Worcestershire in the 1980 and 1981 Annual County Athletic Championships, I was second in the Inter Girls Shot. The English Schools Athletic Association awarded me the Certificate of Merit for Inter Girls Shot champion in the Hereford and Worcester Schools Athletic Championships. I also represented the school at rounders, and I played occasionally for the netball team. But hockey was my first love. I played for Evesham, and my position was goalkeeper. When I was sixteen, I had a moped, and I used to strap my huge pads on the bike as I travelled from fixture to fixture. It was a bizarre sight. I loved being good at something, and I was good at hockey. At the trials for county I beat on points one of the goalkeepers who used to play for England. I'd come top, and that was fabulous.

There was a tough side to me. As goalkeeper I used to love throwing myself around and stopping the ball. It never used to frighten me if I got hit, which I was one time when my friend Judy Elliott split open my eyebrow with a hockey ball, an injury that required seven stitches. Later at Hendon Police Training School I had to jump off the top diving board as part of our swimming test. I didn't like that, but I had to do it. I wasn't fearless, but there were things I'd be happy doing that might have put off other people.

I remember one of the hockey coaches saying to our PT teacher, 'Don't ever let that girl give up goal keeping because she'll make it one day.' It was good to hear. I liked to achieve, and to be acknowledged for my efforts was a welcome bonus. It all felt worthwhile when at secondary school, Prince Henry's High School, Evesham, I was awarded the Special Prize for Services to School Sport on 29 June 1983, which was presented by agony aunt Claire Rayner. In my final year at school, 1983–4, I was deputy head girl, captain of PHHS's First XI, captain of Worcestershire's Second XI, Midlands Trials, and involved in athletics and netball.

No one else in my family is particularly interested in sport. Dad was good at football when he was young and quite a shot in the army, in which he'd served as a conscript. My brother, Peter, though he lives for motorbikes and is a highly skilled civilian mechanic with the army at Ashchurch, is not at all sporty, and neither is my mum. The only sports I recall from my early years are football and wrestling. The former I used to watch with my dad; the latter with Nana, my father's mother. Wrestling on TV was the highlight of her week. Every Saturday afternoon, while my parents were working, she'd come over to keep an eye on us, and we'd sit and watch it together. Every move the wrestlers made, she would imitate, leaping up and down from the sofa, arms and legs flailing. She would get so involved it was risky to sit next to her.

Some Saturday nights I might go out with my hockey friends; four of us used to go around together, drinking in the local pubs. That was as adventurous as it got, apart from the occasional sortie to Marilyn's, the town's nightclub, but I can count on the fingers of one hand the number of times I went there. Clubbing wasn't really me. I didn't like having to get dressed up. I was happier in the pub in my jeans. But I did have ambition. I wanted a career. I didn't want, as I saw it, to waste my life. At school, sport had been everything. I'd become deputy head girl because of my involvement in it. It had got me recognition. Academically I could be lazy and did the bare minimum to get by; my heart was always on the playing-field. And so it came down to a choice between PE teacher-training college and police cadet training school.

I decided on the latter: being a police officer was something in which I believed I could take pride, and my fate was sealed when I answered a recruitment advertisement in the *Express* for the Metropolitan Police Cadets. Though I'd been interested in joining the local force, West Mercia, they had only a skeleton cadet scheme, so I found myself up in London for an extended three-day interview. I went on my own and remember feeling quite panicky, especially about my first trip on the tube. In truth, the thought of it all was terrifying, but it was what I wanted to do so I gritted my teeth and got on with it. Like I always did and always thought I would. It wasn't long before I received the letter of acceptance that was to change my life in ways I could never have imagined, and on 13 August 1984 I emerged from the cocoon of rural Worcestershire.

My initiation into the mean streets of the metropolis was tempered somewhat by my experiences in the Metropolitan Police Cadet Corps and later at Hendon Police Training School. But when I left Childswickham it was with a tremendous sense of purpose. That was just as well, as cadet training was not for the weak or the wayward. When I went back on my first visit to my parents since I'd joined up, I had lost over two stone and was the lightest I'd ever been. It was to be an intense, tiring year that totally preoccupied me, a make-or-break experience that was immensely character-building, challenging and tremendous fun. It was the start of something that would preoccupy me for the next twelve years.

Cadet training school was totally different from anything I'd ever experienced, but once there I immediately got involved. Events took over, and I soon adapted to life in a single-sex dormitory with five other girls. What differentiated our dorm from the boys' were the chintzy bedspreads, one small concession to our gender, of which there were few others, though as you became more senior you got your own room. There was the luxury of our own canteen, though the food was nothing to write home about. Everything else we did ourselves. Not that this went without some financial reward: our wages were the princely sum of £40 a week, but I couldn't believe I got paid for doing something I enjoyed so much. The bonus was that I could save too: I was too busy to spend any of my earnings because the training was so exhaustive and exhausting that I had neither the time nor the inclination to go out.

Going out was further discouraged by the fact that everything else we needed on a day-to-day basis was to hand. Other shared facilities included a segregated shower block, a communal laundry, where you did your own washing and ironing, and the recreation room where you could watch TV or sit around chatting and playing cards. Our intake of cadets was 7/84, and there were twenty-four of us. There was 1/84, 2/84 and so on; I think the late eighties saw the end of the Metropolitan Police Cadets. They were disbanded by the Met a year or so after I was there. You were, of course, very proud of your intake, and for us 7/84 was the best there was. This was very important: to be the best girls, the fittest girls, the smartest girls. Inter-intake rivalry was fierce.

We were issued with a badge with 7/84 printed on it, plus our uniforms, two complete sets: plain black shoes, dark navy-blue trousers, a blue round-neck woollen jumper, pale-blue cravat, rough blue-serge shirt and a blue beret with a white band. There were also assorted exercise kits, including white Fred Perry shirts and the ubiquitous navy-blue gym knickers. Some way into the course the uniform changed to white shirts and a blue policewoman's hat replaced the beret. The hat was important: we wore it all the time, even for the study sessions, though we did take it off in class. The final phase in our rites of passage from the cadets was when we were issued with a blue woollen skirt and fully fledged police jacket. This smart uniform was our final reward.

From the start we were taught how to take care of our uniforms. We had to learn to iron to a required standard: if you didn't reach it you earned a black mark and an early-morning appearance on parade. There was none of that laying your trousers under the mattress and sleeping on them all night to press in the crease. We had wardrobes, and a certain ritual accompanied the hanging of our clothes in them. A clean shirt had to be ironed each day, but it was our trousers that obsessed us, or, more precisely, the exact placing of the crease. These were carefully sewn into the front with two more tiny ones at the back. The trousers would then be steam-ironed flat to complete the taxing process. You were allowed to sew in the crease. Everyone did. Those of us, like me, who couldn't sew got someone else to do it for them.

The immaculate trousers would then be transferred to the wardrobe, though you hardly dared to breathe on them in case you somehow encouraged an unwanted crease anywhere other than right down the middle of each leg. After a night hanging in the wardrobe, you'd carefully slip on the trousers after breakfast, which you'd eat in your tracksuit so as not to undo any of your painstaking work from the night before. Walking downstairs for parade was a real feat: you had to try not to bend your legs and the journey from the dormitory to the parade-ground was hilariously straight-legged though never straight-faced. You would never, ever, sit down in them at this point. You would also have a strip of Sellotape rolled inside out around your fingers, so that you could use the sticky side to remove any, but absolutely any, trace of fluff anywhere on your uniform. We'd all assemble on the edge of the parade-ground, patting one another to remove some tiny white speck that had evaded our eagle eyes. It's comical to recall, but at the time it was deadly serious. We had to be the smartest girls.

And then there were your shoes. These were my speciality. I made up favours here that I'd lost on the trouser-crease sewing. People would queue up to get me to do their shoes for them. On one parade an inspector told me that mine were the best he'd ever seen. I found the process highly therapeutic. I just loved bulling my shoes: spit-and-polish was where I excelled. What you need is a tin of polish with water in the lid and a pair of old cotton knickers, a section wound tightly over your index finger, the rest in your hand, as a duster. You start by wetting the cloth then dipping it in the polish, which has to be black with an occasional layer of brown to make the colour really deep and intense. This you rub into the boots with tiny light circles. The water gives it a fabulous shine. Of course, once you've polished them so the leather is like a looking-glass, woe betide anyone who treads on them. If anyone stood on your toecaps it would take off precious layers of carefully applied polish, and you'd have to start all over again. Equally your walk to the parade-ground required not only that you did not bend your knees — to protect the creases in your trousers — but also that you did not bend your toes and walked with rigid feet to avoid a crack in the bulling at all costs.

We wore our uniforms from Monday to Friday while we were based at Hendon, and went on parade every three or four days. Preparing for this alone was almost a full-time business, given the exacting standards we set ourselves. For gym there was the whitening of our plimsolls to consider too. And lots of other aspects of our appearance. Makeup, for instance, wasn't encouraged: you'd just about get away with a lick of mascara. And the only jewellery allowed was earring studs, not a lot else. Hair had to be off the collar: short or tied up for women, shorn, like in the army, for men. There was a barber on site for this, but one Saturday I went to Hampstead with a friend to a smart hairdressing salon. We both had our colour done, and the colourist tinted my hair very red, especially at the back. In Hendon I spent the rest of the weekend trying to get rid of the alarmingly bright colour in time for Monday-morning parade. I felt it just wasn't suitable. It wouldn't fit in. And I didn't want to stand out like that. My hair has let me down subsequently too. My press file photograph was taken after a swimming lesson, and I hadn't had time to blow-dry my hair. I hoped the photo would be tucked away and never see the light of day, but it was the one that appeared on the front page of the *Daily Mail*, after I was stabbed. It's funny how that photo came back to haunt me and slip through the net of my high standards.

It wasn't all so relentless. We still managed to have fun, a release from the rigours of training, and that used to happen mostly when we got back to the relative tranquillity of the dorm. An old WPC was assigned as matron to keep us in check; we called her Ma'am Wilson. This was standard practice. The male officers we addressed as Sir. In fact, there were a couple of WPCs protecting our virtue, but this particular officer was on duty the night we raided one of the other dormitories in a fake SAS attack, wearing as masks our blue PE knickers, pulled on over our heads, and fully armed with bags of water. Or was it the time we made apple-pie beds? In any case we got caught, and at six the next morning we were on the running-track as punishment.

Right from the word go it was tough; the Cadet Corps was very strict, almost like the army. When based at Hendon we had an earlyish start, around 7 a.m., with parade three or four times a week after a canteen breakfast. At whatever stage of the course you were on, there was always a test, always the pressure to do your best. Intake 7/84 had a ratio of 3:1 male:female. There were initially seven women cadets, one of whom dropped out early on, and eighteen men. This was a higher ratio of women to men than in the actual police force. There was a lot of self-induced pressure and you felt you were constantly under assessment: whether you were suitable, wanting a good report. A constant striving to be good.

A lot of time was spent at weekends getting kit ready for the following week, doing your shoes and uniform, catching up on the washing that a clean shirt every day demands. I used to stay in Hendon over the weekend rather than travel all the way back to Evesham. We'd go to the pub in the evening or spend time in the gym or playing sport, or just watching TV. There wasn't much time for boyfriends, just a social drink or two and the odd flirtation. A couple of the other girls in my intake had boyfriends, but I wasn't really interested at that stage. I didn't welcome the distraction. At school, I'd had one or two boyfriends, but nothing serious. What I was serious about was my career. About that I was very single-minded.

Our intake did everything together for the entire year we were enrolled at Hendon Cadet School, and a tremendous bond was forged within the group, which remains with me to this day. You find out so much about yourself and others in such a tough, disciplined and challenging environment. You discover aspects of yourself that you didn't know you possessed: how you react to what's thrown at you; how to trust, how to observe and make decisions for yourself. How, most importantly, you never give up. The training itself was split into separate phases or modules, which lasted anything from two to six weeks. The Hendon-based physical-fitness training sessions were interspersed with classroom work, mostly social studies. There were arduous outdoor adventure-training periods at a variety of locations all over the country. And there were two practice-based community placements in London, in my case six weeks at the Toynbee

Hall Community Centre in Aldgate, where I worked mostly with old people. It was run by a certain John Profumo, who seemed very likeable when we were introduced. There was a second six-week placement at a day centre for the mentally ill in Willesden Green; it was over December/January, and I recall that I helped to make and decorate Christmas cakes.

There was also the occasional slice of real life. Cadets might be asked to help conduct searches, for weapons and suchlike, and not long after I'd joined we were brought in to assist on an outside investigation being run by the Met. We, that is Intake 7/84 and a few of the other intakes, were bussed in daily, over a two-week period, to a village not far from Brands Hatch in Sussex. It was a cold fortnight, and there was snow on the ground: perfect weather to dig up the grounds of a man rumoured to have hidden gold bullion there. We used spades and metal detectors and generally assisted the officers involved in the investigation. This was Kenneth Noye's acreage, and he was suspected of involvement in the Brinks-Mat bullion robbery of the early eighties, possible money-laundering or disposing of the proceeds. A surveillance team had been working there, and Noye had killed one of them, an undercover PC, John Fordham, when he disturbed one of Noye's dogs during his work in the grounds. Noye had gone to investigate, and ended up stabbing Fordham to death, a crime of which he was subsequently acquitted under the plea of self-defence. I was later at Hornsey with one of the women from the same surveillance team as John Fordham. It was a bad business.

We put in some spadework that fortnight, ultimately finding nothing. While we were there each day we were given lunch in the village hall, and when we first arrived we were even shown round Noye's house. What sticks in my mind are the secret compartments in some of the cupboards, and one of the PCs on the case telling us that when they went into his house Noye's sounds system was poised to play the title track from the James Bond movie *Goldfinger*. The other detail I recall is that officers discovered that the electricity used to heat his swimming pool had been wired up to a supply for an adjacent old people's home. If this were so, it was not in good taste, and neither was his house: ostentatious, to say the least, and only serving to prove that there are some things that money can't buy. At that time Noye was under arrest, and, though eventually released, he has never been far from the headlines. By May 1999, he had lost his fight against extradition from Spain and was back in the UK to stand trial for a road-rage murder on a sliproad of the M25.

The Met broke us in gently — well, perhaps not gently but certainly with great care and attention to detail. It was an exacting time, and was the vital foundation for our future police work, to which, however, there was very little direct reference. What was stressed in our first six-week module based at the Cadet School was getting fit, fitter than we'd ever been in our lives, and I had been fitter than most people all my life. It was that demanding. There was the marching too. We learnt right from the start, sometimes in time to a band or a drum corps. We endured extensive training to reach this peak of excellence, all regularly monitored by PT tests. I still have one of my PT efficiency certificates, dated 27 October, which signs me off with a pass rate of 91.4 per cent in the first-class PT tests. Later we performed gymnastics displays on certain special occasions such as open days, and there were the sports days too.

With gym work I was largely in my element, though I disliked the assault course. This related to the one fear to which I was prepared to admit, but to which I could not and would not give in: heights. We always just did what we had to do. There was no choice. You didn't ever say no. You couldn't opt out of something just because you were terrified. It was the environment, the culture in which you found yourself. This helped you believe in yourself because once you'd done something that frightened you, it made you realise that even if you were scared you could do it. This was all part of what they were trying to teach you: to believe in yourself. Your insides might be saying, 'No!' You might be resisting like mad, but the fact remained that you could do what you had to do, and it was vital that you did. Years later, when I ran towards the man who shot me on that fateful Boxing Day every fibre in my being was screaming, 'No!' What I wanted more than anything was to run away. That was my natural instinct, but your training takes over and instead, bizarrely, you run towards danger.

Back then, in those first weeks in the Cadets, it was the Postman's Walk I particularly dreaded. This was a vertical ladder of telegraph poles that were roped together up to a platform hanging some twenty foot in the air. The idea was that you should walk unaided up the ladder to the platform; there were no handrails or any balancing devices other than your own sense of balance. From here you would swing off ropes into a net, then balance along a tightrope of taut wire that hung linked to a slack rope above. This was the Postman's Walk. The tension you made between the taut wire and the rope was vital; any slacking meant that you'd fall off and plummet to earth. This wasn't life-threatening but none the less alarming and carried an implicit threat of broken bones. There were other high-wire acts: one involved hauling yourself along an impossibly sky-high rope with one foot in a noose-type loop, the other dangling for balance, but even that paled into insignificance beside the Postman's Walk. It was a deliberately understated name for something that was far from mundane in its demands. In retrospect there was a lot of this debunking, rendering harmless something relatively dangerous by calling it something bland and familiar. I guess that is all part of police culture, where the underlying values are intensely macho, and fear is only for sissies. On the subject of naming there was my nickname: giving people nicknames is something that I think occurs more among groups of men than women. In any case from the day I joined the Cadets I was known as Barney, never Helen. Barney was what my mates called me. I was lucky. Some nicknames were more controversial than the shortening of a surname.

Relationships were formalised during sessions in the classroom that focused on developing interpersonal skills. We studied basic psychology and sociology with a concentration on multicultural studies, learning about the differences between people and developing an awareness of others and ourselves. There was continuous assessment but no exams, the point being to help you develop as a person.

The staff at Cadet School included a handful of civilian teachers, who taught the multicultural studies, but the rest were ordinary PCs assigned to instruction duties. Some were specialists in adventure-training, such as our rock-climbing instructor. Though I didn't delight in the rock climbing, I only just tolerated the classroom study. The adventure-training sessions, which came in many guises, included Basic Wales and Advanced Wales, both involving a couple of weeks' mountain- and rock-climbing, abseiling, rope-bridge building across fast-flowing rivers, hill walking and canoeing until you felt your arms would drop off. I enjoyed the ways this tested me: how a hostile environment can hone you, build your character, develop your personality.

Quite early on in the course we were on an overnight camp, carrying all our kit, as usual. It was a freezing week in March, and I had the misfortune to be suffering from an horrendous stomach virus. We set up camp at the back of a farm, but as the night progressed I just got more and more sick, vomiting every half-hour until it was decided that I should be driven back to base to await the others' return. I hated this. I felt so left out. I disliked not being able to finish what I had started. It so went against the grain. Little did I know how much I would have to fight this instinct in years to come and learn to admit defeat gracefully against impossible odds.

Basic Wales was hard but a fabulous experience; Advanced Wales was much tougher and thus infinitely more rewarding. On each occasion we stayed in Betws-y-coed, in a police house that is no longer in use. It was all such an adventure, and I found it hard to believe that we were being paid to do things that other people paid to do. It was a fantastic opportunity. Sometimes I think that a lot of youngsters who get into trouble with the law might benefit from doing some kind of outward-bound course like this. It might just help them to see themselves and life in a different light and set them on a path at the end of which they could make better lives for themselves.

After Basic Wales a group of us went into training for the Ten Tors, a competitive event set on Dartmoor attended by people from a range of professions, including the army, which requires you to climb a selected ten hills over two days. The idea is that you're allocated a certain time to accomplish each particular section of the Ten Tors route and to arrive at each staging post and the destination at specified times. The door to the Land-Rover in which I was travelling to Devon swung open as we drove along the motorway and my untimely exit was avoided only by some quick-witted person grabbing me as I slid out but the whole experience was a fantastic challenge, both physically and mentally. We camped on Dartmoor overnight and walked some fifty miles over the two days, navigating our own route, carrying all our own gear: sleeping bag, tent, cooking equipment, food supplies, a change of clothing, waterproofs. It is a very big and important event and extremely well attended, but is hard going.

I was very fit after that, which was just as well as I'd decided to attempt the Fourteen Peaks in Snowdon, a challenge that requires its participants to climb, in two days, fourteen peaks in the Welsh mountain range each over 2,000 feet, while carrying all their own equipment. I was delighted to discover that I was able to keep up with all the lads at the front of the expedition because I'd been doing so much walking, and was by then adept at it. It was exceedingly tough, but once again a good experience. We went canoeing in the sea off Wales in March. Afterwards, going home in the Land-Rover, one of the other girls cried with the cold. I didn't, but I couldn't blame her: it was perishing. This was the time I slept out on the top of Snowdon in my sleeping bag. In the language of understatement that I was beginning to learn to speak all I'll say is that it was hot during the day and cold at night, with the added challenge of finding a flat piece of ground among the crags on which to sleep. I didn't get much rest at night, but I was so strong that nothing so minor could slow me down.

A year after I had started, in August 1985, it was time to move on. There was the Passing-out Parade, a huge display attended by everyone who mattered, including our friends and families, and the Dining-in Meal, a formal, six-course celebratory supper. I took a couple of weeks' holiday with a few of the other cadets and went to Cornwall, then Corfu. On 2 September 1985 I left the Cadets and started at Hendon Police Training School. It was a date that was to become significant for me. Six years later, in 1991, I was stabbed on that day in early autumn, while on duty in Hornsey, north London. Later, it was the date on which I passed my advanced-driving test, all part of my endless desire to improve and achieve, which seemed all to the good then, whatever the cost.

In those days in the early autumn of 1985, when I had the supreme confidence of youth and inexperience, what struck me was how much less rigorous the PT was than it had been in the Cadets. For a start there was a more low-key attitude towards physical training and health. Some of the female trainees were allowed to progress at quite a low standard of physical fitness. I couldn't believe how lax it was: in the Cadets, conditions had been as strict as they were in the armed forces. Here, the discipline was less strict, the parades were much less rigorous, and in all sorts of ways it was more easy-going. One of the reasons for this was that my new colleagues on Red Intake were generally older and came from all walks of life, only a few drawn directly from the Cadets. Then there was a lot more bookwork, all that law to learn: the Theft Act and myriad legal procedures. I've never studied so hard in my life. It was a huge confidence boost for me, ultimately, because until then I'd considered myself academically inadequate. In fact, it was just that I'd never been sufficiently interested to make the effort. Books and sport don't go together, and you get labelled as a certain kind of person because you like sport.

I was one of around a hundred recruits, and Red Intake was one of several batches of trainee police constables who arrived at Hendon every year. We were all there to learn how to be police officers, and we were about to have a direct experience of what this meant. I'd been there for a couple of months when the Tottenham riots flared in October 1985, sparked by the collapse of a West Indian woman, Cynthia Jarrett, during a police search of her house in Tottenham. She was taken immediately to hospital and certified dead on arrival. The next day urban guerrilla warfare broke out in north London. Some of the TSG, the Territorial Support Group, then called the DSU (District Support Unit), who were on duty at the Broadwater Farm Estate, where the violent epicentre of the riot had developed, used the facilities at the training school to eat, relax and recuperate during their time off. I have a vivid memory of following the development of the riot on the common-room TV with some of the officers who had been there just hours before. I recall how bizarre they found it to watch themselves on screen shortly after they'd returned from the line of fire.

Amongst other horrors, one of their own, home-beat officer PC Keith Blakelock, from Muswell Hill, Hornsey Division, aged forty and the father of three children, was hacked to death with a machete. He had become cut off from his colleagues and trapped by the rioters in part of the warren of raised walkways that comprised the high-rise estate. The police never caught his murderers, nor did the community come forward to help them. Someone was convicted of the crime, but this verdict was overturned on appeal. A year after the riots, in November 1986, a memorial to the dead PC was unveiled by Neil Kinnock at the Muswell Hill roundabout that he patrolled. It was the fifth to be set up by the Police Memorial Trust, and one of only a few that weren't situated where the officer was killed. It was felt too risky to place it at Broadwater Farm.

Pat Kelly, whom I later married, was in the DSU. He had to deal with the bombardment of paving stones and petrol bombs as well as shotgun pellets, some of which caught him in the leg. But it might have been worse: two or more officers were shot, one in the stomach with a revolver bullet. The DSU were shield-trained and wore helmets with visors. They had shots there, but the SOs (Senior Officers) wouldn't give permission to fire, even when police marksmen had in their sights a rioter who was shooting. This was a bone of contention. Pat's worst experience was of being trapped in a police van surrounded by a furious mob who were hacking at it with machetes. He and his colleagues thought they were going to die. But they didn't:

instead they were back at work within a couple of days. Pat was severely traumatised; others witnessed terrible things and underwent great stress. One of the PCs on Keith Blakelock's shield serial, the squad of officers trained to deal with riots and public disorder, was seriously injured, his face chopped with a machete. But there was no recognition of the trauma they suffered when faced with the get-back-to-work attitude.

It all seemed strangely detached from us, yet this was where we were heading. For us, a bunch of fresh-faced, optimistic teenagers, immersed in the great adventure of our first time away from home, it had as much bearing on reality as Jack Warner standing under the blue light in *Dixon of Dock Green* saying a gently knowing, 'Goodnight, all,' has now to life on the streets for the majority of today's police officers.

The first part of the two-year police training started with the twenty-two-week course at Hendon. There, we lived in our own rooms in a series of tower blocks, segregated into male and female floors, though that never bothered me as I was too busy studying and bulling my shoes! There was a canteen for meals, separate from the one used by the cadets. If the Cadet Corps was like boarding-school, then the Recruits was like college. Instead of a college scarf, though, we wore full police uniform, but any insignia was prefaced with the initials TS, Training School. In the twenty-two weeks we were there we never went out on the streets, but it was here that we learnt all the basics of how to survive there as a police officer. Everything from points of law through role-play — how to deal with a drunk or someone accused of theft — to the boredom, for me, of administrative procedures, including the marginally less tedious strategy of a breathalyser test. The day we were taught how to do this did not turn out quite the way we'd imagined. Our instructor brought in some whisky so that we could experiment with tiny tots to see when the green turned to red, but the tiny tots were not tiny enough, and the entire class degenerated into hilariously drunken chaos.

Our week was mostly an orderly Monday to Friday, with continuous assessment every Monday morning, failure at which prevented your transition to the next stage. It was highly intensive, and I rarely went away at weekends because that was when I had to put in the study time I needed to achieve a pass grade each Monday. There was always the fear of not making it. That drove me. Some people went away from Friday night to Monday morning and crammed their studies into half an hour. They would quite possibly get the same grade as me, even though I'd been working in my room the whole weekend. What a swot! But I couldn't do it any other way. I just had to stay there and study because I didn't want to fail. I can be extremely lazy, and when I think back to my O levels I did the bare minimum. But now that I was doing what I really wanted, I put everything into it. It was important: I wanted to do well. At school I'd been an acclaimed goalkeeper for Evesham in hockey. Now I had a goal of my own to score.

In the middle of all this, there was a death in my family: Gran, my mother's mother who had lived in the caravan in our back garden since I was a year old. It affected me deeply: I had been close to her. I told our class instructor about it, and he was happy to grant me a couple of days' compassionate leave. He also took the opportunity to tell me how very fond of me he was. I found his solicitousness over-friendly and a bit threatening. I felt he had overstepped his boundaries, and it frightened me because he was my teacher. I didn't need that sort of pressure from a married man who was my superior, in a position of authority. But there was little time to worry about this or, indeed, to grieve: I just had to carry on. The course wasn't going to stop for me. This was the unsentimental culture in which I now found myself, and I was beginning to be affected by it. Grin and bear it. Don't give in to your feelings. Stiff upper lip and carry on. I wanted what the Met had to offer so I believed there was no compromise.

Apart from classroom work, there was still PT twice a week and PT tests. I achieved the required a mile and a half in under thirteen minutes for a woman with no great effort, just a degree of dedication. Some of the other students in Red Intake used to laugh when they walked past me as I was doing laps of the running-track on a Friday night when they were on their way to the pub. Sometimes I'd join them later or, if not, on Monday morning they'd greet me with 'You're mad. We saw you on Friday. You're crazy. Why didn't you join us for a drink?' but it was clear that their comments were tinged with admiration. I really got into running around 1991; until then I'd concentrated mostly on gym work. I was even running when I was six months' pregnant with my second child, Molly, but I had to stop soon after that as it became too painful. When I was pregnant with my firstborn, Ben, I trained in the gym and swam throughout. The fact is I've always been involved with sport and keeping fit: it gets addictive after a while.

Which is how I found police work once I got out on the

street. During your time at Hendon you look just like a fully fledged police officer, but it is not until you receive your warrant card and are assigned to a station that you can begin to live that image. In January 1986 I was posted to Hornsey police station in north London. When I left Hendon Police Training School I did so with more than I'd bargained for with that Baton of Honour for Top Recruit. At the Passing-out Parade I was presented with a commemorative wooden and metal tipstaff. A precursor to the truncheon, constables' tipstaves were initially used by the Bow Street Runners in the 1750s and largely replaced by the truncheon with the formation of the Metropolitan Police in 1829. It was a great honour. And my name is up there now in Reception at Hendon on the Scroll of Honour. I've been back a couple of times, and I admit that it always thrills me to see myself there.

But however glorious my departure, however much my reputation was enhanced by it, and others were anticipating my brilliant career, I didn't have a clue what life as a serving police officer was going to involve, despite all my eighteen months of training. Of course, I wasn't aware of this at the time. All I did know was that I was to live at Tottenham section house in Northumberland Road, two miles from Hornsey police station. All I knew about Tottenham was the riots.

CHAPTER 3

BIG CITY BEAT

It was a death by hanging in the stairwell of a small white stucco townhouse at an address in Jackson's Lane, Highgate. This is a leafy, upmarket area of north London, five minutes' walk from the green spaciousness of Hampstead Heath, its streets lined with terraces of desirable Georgian, Victorian and Edwardian properties. I'd been on foot patrol near Queen's Wood when a colleague picked me up in a divisional Panda and raced off along Shepherd's Hill, screeching through the lights on red at the busy Archway Road junction. The call was to a sudden death, so I was puzzled by the urgency. Surely we weren't going to miss anything; no one was going anywhere. The gentility of the area contrasted sharply with the reality that faced us once we were admitted to the house: a suicide by hanging is never a pretty sight.

When I walked in I logged the grimness of the scene, but my training, everything I'd been taught at Hendon as a cadet and a recruit, took over, as well as my own desire never to fail or let the side down. I knew it was not only unprofessional but also unacceptable to show my feelings. Even in those very early days I was tough and capable, resilient enough never to be a wilting lily. I just closed down my natural responses and got on with the job.

With a sudden death there's always a lot of waiting time, so there was nothing sudden about our departure. There was the doctor to call to certify the death, then the coroner's officer to decide whether or not an inquest or post-mortem was required and to authorise the removal of the body to a mortuary by a firm of undertakers. My colleague Paul Storey stayed with me, fortunately one of life's nice people and an officer I liked and respected. If possible you need to pick your companions carefully in such circumstances. A sudden death is something that needs to be handled sensitively. All the textbooks tell you that it is a distressing ordeal for everyone concerned, not just for the immediate family, that police officers can come to terms with it, but that the experience can be damaging if not handled correctly. They stress that it is important to keep an eye on yourself as it can have a considerable effect on you, that you may need to talk about it with other, more experienced officers or even seek qualified help.

It wasn't something I ever discussed with anyone, and I was aware of little of this as I kept my vigil over the corpse. What I did notice was a drop on his nose turn slowly into a translucent trail, like an unwoven strand of a spider's web. I had no idea how he'd become ensnared in the web of delusion that had driven him to take his own life, but I was very young and trying hard not to be affected by it.

Whatever else you do, you don't cut them down. You leave that for the undertaker, who would always cut the rope rather than untie the knot. The kind of knot tied might be important later. In any case it took some time for them to turn up, shortly after the coroner's officer had gone. Apart from observing the ever-increasing line of slime that ran so unstoppably from the dead man's nostril, I spent my time taking all the notes you need to make on such occasions, anything relevant, but mostly mundane — bizarrely so, given what had happened. What was the deceased wearing? What kind of knot had he used to secure the noose on the rope he used to kill himself? CID had to be informed, and there were all manner of bureaucracies through which to proceed.

Sudden deaths aren't all about suicide. Sometimes there's a collapse behind closed doors that can happen for a variety of reasons and with a range of outcomes. One I remember was a few years on, when I was accompanying a probationary police constable. We accepted a call on our PR, the personal radio with which each of us was issued. It took us to a council estate in Wood Green. Death does not distinguish between classes, and this is an area of London as far from Highgate socially as the Mall is from Mile End; nevertheless it still fell under the remit of Hornsey Division. Wood Green, a largely poor and deprived urban district, was top of the crime ratings for the division. There were a lot of muggings, car thefts, armed robberies and burglaries, especially on and around the High Road. The area has a high level of social problems, which manifest themselves in crime, things that the average person doesn't see, and neither had I until then. One of the less attractive aspects of life as a police officer is that you tend to see all the bad. When I was first patrolling the streets of Hornsey, I was astonished by the number of heavy metal shutters that were pulled down over the front of shops when they closed up at night. In those days we just didn't have anti-crime devices like that back home. There were lots of other, similar things that I noticed, but the hardest part was accepting what people were capable of doing to each other.

The old boy who lived in the flat to which we'd been called had not been seen for some days. As I was puppy-walking the young probationer — the name given to the job of street duties with a rookie PC — I was the one who took charge and forced a window to climb through when we noticed the drawn curtains and the lack of response to our knock.

It was a warm summer day, but the stench that hit me as I clambered down off the sill into a small bedroom was not only due to lack of ventilation in hot weather. When he had suffered his heart-attack and slumped to the floor, the pensioner had fallen on to an electric fire that he must have had turned up to its highest setting. By the time I found him, his body was black and rotting, slowly cooking. I managed to stop myself from gagging as I stepped across him and out through the bedroom to the hallway, where I opened the street door to the young PC. It was horrendous, but I couldn't give any sign of how much it had affected me. I was showing a junior officer the ropes so it was a matter of professional pride — it's just not done to display any sign of weakness. I had to preserve my seasoned-officer mask. We concentrated on practical matters. We had to identify the dead man, not always easy because neighbours often aren't much help in these cases. Frequently in London people don't know their neighbours. Or they know each other too well, are over concerned with one another, and end up in disputes. Parking across driveways to cause an obstruction is a favourite revenge in the catalogue of neighbours behaving badly.

But this was a prime example of urban neglect, which in the early days I found incomprehensible and distressing. After a while, you become a bit desensitised. In a way you have to in order to survive because, though sudden deaths like these are certainly not run-of-the-mill, you're dealing with similar incidents all the time. Usually they're just part of the job. Until the day, that is, when something extraordinary happens to you, and then they're not. For me that day had not yet arrived. I was just starting out and eagerly took on everything the job threw at me, good and bad.

When I first went out on the streets I felt that the whole

world was looking at me. Please, God, I prayed, don't let me have to deal with anything. I was being puppy-walked by a confirmed PC, but there was nothing about my appearance that would identify me to the general public as new to the job, so when the worst happened and someone approached me I knew there was no way out. I looked like a police officer, now I must behave like one. My heart was in my mouth; I hoped the ground would swallow me up. What on earth could they want? Would I be able to help them? Would they realise this was my first day and the first question I'd ever been asked in my new role? Help, help, help! My mind raced. I wanted to hide behind my streetwalker and inwardly started to shake. As I registered the question, I almost fell about laughing with relief: Did I know the way to . . . ? It was ever thus.

It could have been worse. PC Henry Wood joined up on 25 March 1834. His initiation involved the issue of his uniform at Scotland Yard, a walk to Poplar police station, to which he had been posted, and a day in which his duties were explained to him. The following night he could be seen walking his beat from the Ferryhouse Mill as a fully fledged constable. No cadet school, no Hendon recruit training. Just get on with it the best he could. In my case for best read worst, because right from the word go I was told I was too nice to the public. But you soon learn to adapt not only to what your job wants you to be but also to what you've got to be to work well as a good police officer and to survive. You begin not to accept people at face value, to look deeper, and you don't believe everything anyone tells you any more. From being a trusting person, I had to learn not to trust anyone. In the early days I encountered people I'd never met the like of before: armed robbers and con men, drug addicts and wife beaters, mentally ill people thrown on to the streets by Care in the Community and those just desperate and at the end of their tether. These weren't circles in which I'd ever moved.

As a probationary police constable I had arrived with an image of what it was going to be like out in the real world, doing a real job as a PC. Neither the Cadets nor the Recruits can prepare you for that. The training there is a basic survival kit, to put you on your feet. When you are assigned to your first posting and finally learn to put one foot in front of the other, reality, the street outside, the station inside, can be a letdown. I'd found myself working in an urban culture that was at the opposite end of the social spectrum from the rural community from which I'd come. Fortunately I could handle the contrasting worlds. But they were different. It wasn't just the armoury on the street, the metal shutters over the shop-fronts at night. It was something that affected the inner workings for the force.

Of course, the police represent a cross-section of society and, as in the world outside, most of the people in the force are lovely, just nice and totally ordinary. There are the characters and the eccentrics, who add colour, like Harry the Dog. He was an older PC, who had a glove puppet that he engaged in conversation with prisoners in the charge room and the station cells. He was a big, beefy, ex-Navy man, who used to amuse himself and any station inmates, his captive audience, thus. But there were a few things that were not so beguiling, aspects of the Met culture that I could at best only tolerate, but about which I had to put up and shut up.

Among them were colleagues who set a tone around the

place and within the Met that I found hard to stomach. The canteen culture was one such element I disliked. I remember being shocked by some of my colleagues, the continual swearing, the crude and sexist comments. I hadn't expected this, but I soon absorbed it as part of everyday life. It became the norm, but I always determined from the start that none of this would change me. I would never become like that. Obviously, certain aspects of my character had to change to some extent for me to be a better police officer, but the canteen culture was out of bounds to me. There was one canteen lady, Rose, who bantered with the men, giving back as good as she got, but I didn't want to be like that.

I was lucky in that I would get involved in anything that any of the men could do. I could chase suspects, run after them as well as any man. On one occasion in the middle of the night a colleague and I stopped two young men in a car. One of them ran off, and I pursued him over half a mile, keeping control posted on my PR. Eventually it all gelled, and he was nicked.

I used to say you needed to maintain a certain level of fitness so that, at worst, you could run away and save your life one day. But some officers let themselves go. It wasn't just about being physically fit: some PCs were just lazy, fat and overweight, and couldn't run even to save their own lives. They didn't want to get involved, wouldn't answer calls or give chase to any escaping prisoner. They would seize any opportunity for indoor duty. Some people weren't cut out to be a police officer. I accept that there were aspects of the job at which I didn't excel, and I had my lazy days, but it is largely an attitude of mind and body. I was still going to the gym on a daily basis, in Edmonton, where

I was lifting massive weights. I could squat and lift over 120kg. I was really strong, which was all part of my capable image. Looking back I see this to be so. In some ways this conspired against me, because no one ever worried about me: Helen can cope, she's tough. And I was. But not superhuman.

Another time, when I was a probationer on foot patrol with a parent constable, we accepted a call to a local building society. A man had been detained there by staff because of suspicions about the card he was presenting to withdraw cash. We talked to the suspect for a while, and through the control room at Hornsey we did a routine PNC, Police National Computer check, on him — name, age, sex, colour, height, always in that order. It came up negative. But we decided to arrest him anyway. It was my arrest; as a probationer I needed to do it for the Record of Work that charted my progress. As we emerged from the building society and out on to the street, he decided to make a run for it. I raced after him. On my PR I reported what was happening, and eventually we caught up with him and arrested him again. It was only later that I discovered the name he'd given was false, and that if we'd known who he really was the computer would have informed us that he was wanted for armed robbery. Without realising it, I had put myself in a position of some considerable personal danger, which was reflected in a favourable arrest report. Without meaning to boast, I'm not sure that knowing about his record would have put me off giving chase. Once I'd got on the case, nothing would have stopped me.

All this probably helped me to avoid the major pitfalls of station bullying and harassment. I became well respected, not that I got on with everyone but I was professionally well thought of, with consistently good reports. This all made it easier for me. If I'd been a WPC who was seen to be not up to scratch, not very capable, I think my life would have been very different, as it would have been for any male PC who was felt not to be pulling his weight. Nevertheless, there are few allowances for gender and, given the nature of the job, it is a tough world that promotes a macho culture.

You had to know when to let things go. Graham Mansfield, now a friend, was a sergeant on my relief. I was in the driving seat, he was my operator, and we were chatting in a Panda parked in the station yard. I had my PR clipped to my shoulder, and it started to crackle into life, making one hell of a din. Graham couldn't hear a word I was saying so he leant over to turn down the volume. Instead of pressing the radio's volume-control switch he accidentally made contact with my breast. He took his hand away as if he'd been electrocuted and mumbled an immediate apology. He was incredibly embarrassed. I thought it was funny, though he was never allowed to forget it. I met Graham again, years later, when he was a sergeant at Catford, south-east London, and I was in the ARVs. We'd been called to his division to deal with an armed incident, which had dissipated by the time we arrived. There I was in full body armour with my gun deployed when a huge, six foot five, officer came running towards me shouting, 'Darling.'

The others looked askance at him. 'Do you know her?' they asked.

'Oh, yes,' he replied, 'and she's still gorgeous.' He didn't try to turn down my radio that time. But it is not always so light-hearted. Take the case of WPC Anna-Maria Robb, reported by the *Daily Mail* in May 1998. One of her chief constables made what she described as crude and insensitive remarks about the size of her breasts at a mess evening, an allegation the officer denied. But WPC Robb only dropped her claim for sexual discrimination after reaching a settlement with the police force.

There was one PC, older than the rest, who was just obnoxious. What used to come out of his mouth had to be heard to be believed. He was rude to WPCs in general and, depending on his mood, to the public. One night we attended a domestic, and a neighbour leant out of an upstairs window to see what was going on. Unprovoked, he told them to fuck off. We all thought, Oh, typical, and shrugged it off, but when he turned it on you, as a WPC you just took it, because you didn't feel you were in any position to do anything about it. It was difficult to accept, but he got away with years of being abusive to other people. I was determined to let nothing, especially the likes of him, undermine my desire to do my best in my chosen career, but I didn't know when I joined the Met exactly what I was letting myself in for. This was probably just as well.

The shoulder number I was given when I arrived at Hornsey in February 1986 was 824YR. This number may change as you move from station to station, but you will always have your warrant number. It is unique to you and for life: PC007205 was mine; it's almost tattooed on my heart. The fact is that I had entered a profession that I was to live and breathe for the next ten years. I had found something I really wanted to do and I would stick with it, for better and for worse. It was almost till death us do part.

Hornsey police station is in Tottenham Lane. It's a

traditional-looking red-brick building with a blue lamp, everyone's image of a model nick, like those in fifties films such as *The Lavender Hill Mob*, which came out of Ealing Studios just after the war. It was purpose-built in the early 1900s and had endured an assortment of extensions but remained as attractive as these buildings get. A lot of the new stations are built to look like Pizza Hut — in fact that's what we christened the one in Uxbridge. The area headquarters at Edmonton were new and built over a natural spring, which caused no end of problems; the area itself comprised Enfield, Edmonton, Tottenham and Hornsey. I was on Hornsey Division during the eighteen months that remained of my probationary period and for almost nine years of my career. The division was split into four sections: Hornsey, Wood Green, Highgate and Muswell Hill — from the sublime to the ridiculous, with areas of extreme poverty abutting those of extreme wealth in that unique social mix that is London.

We were to experience a taste of how our lives would go from now on when four of us new probationers drove down from Tottenham section house to Hornsey together that first day in February in one lad's brand-new Polo. We parked in a nearby side-street. Dressed in half uniform, wearing our own jackets over the regulation issue, we walked the five minutes it took to reach Tottenham Lane and the station. When we returned at the end of the day, it was to discover that the car had been vandalised, with several long, malicious scratches engraved into the mirror-like bodywork. It was a sign of things to come, an indication of the area in which we were working, and possibly of how some of the residents felt about us. No one had told us it was going to be easy.

That first day, and for the next week, we worked nine to five, based in the station for the induction period, learning the ropes, getting the lie of the land and discovering the bureaucracy that underpins police street work. It never ceased to amaze me how long it took to do paperwork; for example, in an arrest, you could spend ten minutes one afternoon arresting someone, and the rest of the day filling in the forms integral to the arrest procedure. Paperwork never was my favourite part of the job, and in those pre-computer days it was all pen-and-paper work. I'm a very active person, and there was more paperwork than I'd bargained for. I thought I'd never get to grips with it. A few years later I was off sick for several months, the sole benefit of which was that all my outstanding paperwork was divided out among my colleagues. I returned to a blissfully empty in-tray.

On arrival we reported to the street duties sergeant and were introduced to the other PCs. I was assigned a locker and shown around: the loos, the showers, the canteen; the administrative offices upstairs, the station office — these days manned by support civilians. To digress slightly, I have to say that to my mind this is not a healthy progression. Although part of the trend away from PCs being too office-bound is something with which I agree. Perhaps I am old-fashioned but I think that if you walk into a police station you have a reason for doing so, and I can imagine that it might be somewhat offputting to be met by a civilian, with no police officer in sight. In the mid-eighties, walkers often manned the office, though rarely the drivers, who were too valuable to be taken off patrol.

Hornsey, along with Wood Green, was a charging station, so there were cells and later, with the advent of tape-recorded interviews, properly equipped interview rooms. The days passed in a flurry of form-filling and kit allocation, including handcuffs and weaponry, such as it was. Everyone has batons or asps now, made of light alloy, gravity fed with a ratchet action that is highly effective, but then it was a thick light-coloured wood cudgel about as long as your forearm. The women's standard-issue truncheon was smaller than the men's, but even so mine wouldn't fit into the special truncheon pocket sewn into the side seam of my trousers. My trousers were just too tight; all that gym work had built up my muscles. Any officer who uses the asp has to state their reasons for doing so, just as with CS spray. But I couldn't even get my truncheon in my pocket, so mostly I didn't bother to take it out with me. It was a good job my leg muscles were in such good shape, because at least I had the option of running away if things got too tough.

In that first week there were endless instructions and introductions followed by a macabre interlude: the routine probationers' visit to the local mortuary, in our case Middleton Road, Hornsey, to witness a post-mortem. It was grim but comically macabre, with most of the other inhabitants of the room dead, mostly old, some headless. It was a relief when we were finally let out on street duties with puppy-walkers to hold our hands. On the whole these more senior officers were very helpful, though there were stories that have turned into legend about how the more experienced officers initiated the raw PCs into Met life.

I think I was lucky, because the worst I experienced was an eccentric PC, who, maybe because of my youth and inexperience, thought he was dealing with a child, which enabled him to behave like one. In any case he insisted that we were not to tread on any of the lines between the paving stones, only the squares, otherwise we'd be eaten by monsters. I remember walking down the street with him as he avoided all the cracks. It was hilarious, though I was puzzled by it. Now I realise that he was just letting off steam in what is fundamentally a stressful and demanding job, where you have sometimes to let go and be a bit daft and childish as a foil for all that relentless responsibility.

There was room for fun later too. Not long after I'd been assigned to my divisional team, B-Relief, one snowy February evening a few of the B-Relief PCs found themselves up on the steep, grassy slopes of the hill that leads up to Alexandra Palace in Muswell Hill. It was a really quiet night, and the park, all 480 acres of it, was deserted and covered in a thick crisp layer of virgin snow. It was too tempting to resist: we threw professional caution to the wind and spent hours sledging down the hill on our shields and black bin liners. It's something I'll never forget.

Making fun at someone else's expense is sometimes a less attractive proposition, but probationers are prime candidates for the wind-up, and there was always someone ready to have a go at any of the new arrivals who didn't fit in. One new PC's behaviour was a little on the loud side, which tended to grate on some of the more experienced officers. The plan to bring him down a peg or two involved him accepting a hoax night call to Highgate Woods. There he was pounced on by a few of the duty officers and tied to a tree. Thus restrained his trousers were pulled down to his ankles and his body smeared all over with black boot polish. They left him like that for hours: there he stayed at the mercy of the elements and midnight ramblers. It was a standard rite of passage of the kind that is no longer permitted, which is probably just as well because although most such pranks were meant as a joke there was always one that was more sinister and undermining.

Some probationers were just plain gullible, like the new PC who was sent to the chemist to collect what he thought was medication for a prisoner. Much to his embarrassment the custody officer had written 'packet of condoms' on the note he presented to the pharmacist. And then there was the PC who got involved in the supposed Annual Truncheon Training Trials, located in a remote part of the division, lit by the headlights of the vans and panda cars. The idea, he was told, was that you should throw your truncheon as far as you could then retrieve it and try again. His one and only throw ended in a night's search through an adjacent wood, now unlit due to the departure of everyone else from the scene. He searched without success through a dense tangle of brambles and undergrowth for most of the night.

I got caught myself from time to time, once after I'd arrested the man who turned out to be an armed robber. One afternoon my reporting sergeant, Danny Keogh, collared me in the canteen to tell me he'd received a complaint from two nuns about my behaviour that day. They had taken exception to hearing me swear at the suspect during the incident and had written a letter to say so. Danny looked very grim when he handed it to me, and he did all this with such a straight face that it wasn't until days later that I realised he had written the letter himself and that the whole of my relief were in on it. Though I didn't know it at the time, part of my luck in avoiding some of the worst outrages perpetuated against raw PCs was down to the quality of the reputation that preceded me. The fact that I'd been awarded the Baton of Honour meant that great things were expected of me, and I received a degree of respect for this. Years later a friend told me that this was the word on the ground. That was the impression people had of me, though I was not aware of it at the time. But in those early days the biggest transition I made was from the station to the street at the end of the first week, to spend the next six weeks on foot patrol. During this time I experienced the full gamut of the beat police.

As probationers we were given all the jobs that no one else wanted to do. This reflected the station hierarchy with the relief inspector, usually a man, at the top, several sergeants, probably six or seven, below him, and then the police constables. There was a pecking order within the PCs, which found the probationers at the bottom, traditionally dumped on but in the process learning a wide range of skills. It has all changed now, but learning was the principle behind it: you started at the bottom, walking to all calls. As probationers we did all the sudden deaths, standing on premises that were insecure, always on foot patrol. It was a good learning curve.

Burglary was almost an everyday call-out. You'd enter each and every incident in the burglary book at the station's crime desk, where there was also the motor-vehicle book, for car theft or any other car crime; the major-crime book for certain classified crimes, such as grievous bodily harm, arson and murder. Finally there was the beat-crime book, for everything that did not fit any of these categories. Quite often on your shift you would simply go out and walk or drive around. On nights you could be more proactive because there was less crime to process, and you had time to stop more people, but on a typical day shift you'd go out and not look back, going from one call to another, reporting incidents that had already happened. We would take details of a crime in our pocketbooks for transfer to the relevant crime-report book — before computerisation this was how it was done. From here a decision would be made about the next stage, if there was to be one. The sad fact is that a lot of crime is recorded, and that's as far as it goes.

You would get called out to an armed robbery, even if you weren't armed. I used to think that this was slightly bizarre. There you'd be, breaking your neck to get to some incident where someone was reported to be holding a hostage at bay with a shotgun. You'd be driving frantically through heavy London traffic, wondering what you would do if they were still in the vicinity, armed and dangerous, when you got there. Usually they'd be gone by the time you arrived, but if it was something like an armed siege, an unarmed officer would be the first port of call, although the Firearms Unit would be called out too. Our job as beat PCs was to contain the incident at a safe distance, to make sure that the public were not at risk.

Sometimes the public proved very wearing, not so much in major incidents such as these but more so on an everyday level. We got called out regularly to sort things that didn't merit our attention, and I'd think it incredible that someone had phoned the police over something minor like an argument about a parking space. Who did they think we were?

Domestics can be very tiresome and no-win. I can remember reflecting at the beginning, when I was only nineteen or twenty, that I was dealing with domestic strife, occasionally quite violent, that involved people of the same age as my parents. I didn't have sufficient experience of life to tell them what's what and sort out their problems.

Some police work was more straightforward. I found a photo of myself the other day taken in July 1986 at the wedding of Prince Andrew and Sarah Ferguson, now the Duchess of York. In it I'm wearing my full uniform and standing next to the man who was then one of the most highly decorated officers in the Met: Ryan David, who'd been awarded the Queen's Gallantry Medal. I was a very new probationer then, not even twenty. I found it extremely exciting to be on duty in central London at an occasion of such pomp and circumstance. For once everyone was happy and relaxed, and we mingled with the crowd. At one point we were rooted to the spot for so long that we got to know the couple standing next to us. In an extraordinary coincidence it turned out that they were from Banbury and knew my parents from the fruit and vegetable stall that they ran in the market there. It was they who took the photos of Ryan David and me, which they gave to my mum in Banbury a few weeks later.

The following year I was involved in a drama of a different kind: the aftermath to that October's Great Storm. Haringey Council had called us in to help to clear up the massive damage. One PC got hold of a chainsaw and became expert at sawing up fallen trees into logs. On early turn as a lowly probationer I stood the whole morning on Shepherd's Hill, turning back traffic from a vital through road that had been turned into a cul-de-sac by a huge wind-felled tree. It was chaos that day, absolute mayhem, but we mucked in where needed. Sometimes that took us out of our division.

There was the ambulance-drivers' dispute in 1989. We

did our best to take over their role, and, working with the army, we took the ill and injured to hospital in the army's Green Goddesses. I did a special training course for that and worked as a medic. We also got posted to Wapping to assist on the dispute there. Nothing dramatic, just a line of us blocking off a road while a bunch of protestors marched by. A chap came up to me and presented me with a bunch of half-wilted roses. I don't where he'd come from, out of the pub perhaps. I felt really embarrassed, and I can't think that I stood there and held them. There was a lot of bad feeling towards the police in Wapping, so this was an unusual gesture. I have to say that while I was on duty men would sometimes ask me out. Just joking around, they'd invite me on a date, trying to get my guard down and have a laugh with me. My colleagues used to tease me about it, but I took it in good heart.

What I also developed a reputation for, which peaked a few years into the job, was my high arrest level. There's so much crime around that it was easy to walk out of the police station and arrest somebody. We used to have a laugh about it as I went out, and I'd say to my sergeant, 'I'm off now. See you in half an hour.' So we'd go out, drive around for a bit, spot somebody suspicious, stop them and quite often go on to arrest them. Drug crimes, such as possession of cannabis or ecstasy tablets, are very common. One night we stopped a car in which there was a group of young lads. They'd reacted oddly when they saw us: their body language gave them away. It turned out they had a stash of ecstasy that they tried to hide down the car seats. As they got out, a bag dropped on to the road and split, the tablets rolling into the gutter.

It is said that most jobs contain a high percentage of

boredom, and life as a PC in the Met is no exception. There was the paperwork, and there were the quiet days when you just reported incidents that had already happened, such as burglaries, stolen cars, thefts from cars, trivial domestics. No one ever told me there were days like these. There were even days when nothing happened at all, but these were few and far between. After six weeks' foot patrol, I was assigned to B-Relief. We operated in shifts: early turn, 6 a.m. to 2 p.m.; late turn, 2 p.m. to 10 p.m.; nights, 10 p.m. to 6 a.m. Shiftwork is a killer, not only the antisocial hours but also the constant disruption to your body clock. When I started in the mid-eighties, shifts were organised in a four-week pattern. You would do, say, seven days of nights, then late turn, which meant a quick changeover, in which you'd get home between 6.30 and 7 a.m., go to sleep, get up, dress and eat, and come back in again for 2 p.m. After the two days off that followed you'd be on earlies.

As you go through your probationary period, the pressure is on you. You need to be seen to be active. Although it's technically difficult to sack anyone, as I've already said, I wanted to do well and be seen in a good light. As time went by, I got a bit worn down, and shift work combined with increasing responsibility can prove exhausting. Doing nights at first is fun. I remember driving back to Tottenham section house early one morning and thinking how nice it was that I'd finished work and could sleep and relax all day while everyone else was about to get up and get going. But your priorities change, as they did for me, especially after my son, Ben, was born, a few years later. Then your time's not just for you, and you get tired. Things become a bit much. You hardly have time to draw breath, never mind conduct a social life.

This is probably why so many police marry each other or live together. You don't meet many people outside work, and those you meet during the course of it do not encourage you in your appreciation of the human race. The nature of the job makes you somewhat cynical about your fellow man, dealing as you do, day in, day out, with the largely antisocial elements of the community.

I began to develop a sixth sense about people. It was just a gut feeling that I can't rationalise. Quite often I'd have an overwhelming need to talk to a certain person, stop a particular car or investigate something that caught my eye. I was usually right. Not always, or I'd be fêted in wreaths of glory. It was something that developed over the time I was in the force. If it was someone on foot, I would explain my reasons for stopping them: the Police and Criminal Evidence Act 1986 sets out the rules that apply when you stop a person or search a vehicle. You would know within a couple of minutes whether or not your instincts were correct: body language, computer and document checks would bear them out or not. But the bottom line is that you get used to dealing with people. Experience builds your sixth sense, if you're prepared to take notice of it.

When I'd arrived at Hornsey, I was largely an unknown quantity. Everyone expected things of me, partly because of the Baton of Honour, but no one knew how I would perform on the street. As time went by I began to prove myself, and slowly but surely people became aware that I was quite good at the job. What makes a good officer is a mixture of a range of qualities that include the ability to communicate and a degree of confidence in what you do. It was felt that I had this, and a willingness to get my hands dirty.

If you were bad at your job, you stood out; equally so, if you were good at it. My inspector would comment on how I was always smiling and ready to get involved, in fights or skirmishes, prepared to run towards an incident rather than away from it. I was willing and eager. I liked to have a go. Inevitably you get hurt along the way, but I was prepared for that. There's some damage you don't reckon on, though, where the price is too high.

Even when you thought you were safest, back at base, you were still at risk. Once I had a run-in with a colleague's violent female prisoner, a Nigerian woman arrested on deception charges. Correct procedure required that a WPC should be in attendance during her finger-printing, and I was asked to help. Now, it must be said that when it comes to violence a woman can be just as vicious as any man, and this one was no exception. Normally fingerprinting is a delicate operation, in which you stand behind the person whose prints are being taken to hold their fingers and roll them gently, one by one, over the ink block before printing them in the ruled boxes on a sheet of paper. Any difficulty in fulfilling this routine procedure and the rulebook allows you to use reasonable force.

To put it mildly, this woman would not co-operate, and in fact she was behaving very aggressively, flailing around furiously, hitting out at whoever came near her. Along with a couple of male officers, I found myself with my arms wrapped around her in a reluctant, restraining embrace, during which she decided to use the last deterrent remaining to her. In her final act of revenge she sank her teeth into my upper arm and bit down hard into my flesh. She must have been charged with assault on a police officer, because I've still got the photographs they took as evidence, a practice when injury is incurred in the line of duty.

As a WPC you had special responsibilities related to your gender. For example, there was a time when we had to guard all the B11 Home Office prisoners who were farmed out to police stations during a prison authorities' dispute. Muswell Hill, although no longer a charging station, still had its cells, and these B11 prisoners, the majority of whom were women, were held there. We WPCs, in turn, had to accompany a sergeant to attend the station as a jailer. If you were on early turns you had to give them their breakfast; later in the day there were visits to organise. I didn't enjoy this aspect of the job. It wasn't why I'd joined the Met.

In these early days it was all par for the course. Perhaps I should have welcomed the respite. But I enjoyed a challenge. I was happy and optimistic, and not worn down by the successive traumas that are part and parcel of police life, threatening not only physical health but also emotional well-being. But even a cat has only nine lives. And how many life-threatening situations can you survive?

From autumn 1985 to summer 1987 I had regularly — as often as once a month — to sit probationers' exams, each of which I had to pass to move on to the next stage. My final exam was on 9 June 1987. I passed, and was confirmed as a police constable. By this time I'd been at Hornsey for eighteen months, and it was Yippee! I'd reached my goal. It felt magical to know that I was now officially part of the Met. I felt wonderful. Life was going my way. I really believed that. And never more so than in the following year when I passed the standard police-driving course, a two-week intensive run at Hendon. I achieved this within three years of joining up, which, apparently, was impressively fast. I was on an upward flight and beginning to feel unstoppable.

To be a police driver is something you aim for. It represents the next step up the career ladder. I could now drive the Metro Panda cars, and while I was at it I passed the van course for good measure. That meant I could drive the Sherpas, too, the vehicles that were used to pick up prisoners. This was all a big step up from being a walker, especially as I had somehow managed to come top of my class. My instructors were glowing in their assessment of my abilities and suggested I should go on to take the advanced driving course immediately. This was something for which normally you had to wait a couple of years. However, an opportunity to do it didn't present itself, because there were no places available on the courses that were about to start, and it wasn't until 1994 that I became an advanced driver. I still had reason to feel proud, though, I hadn't set out to get the highest mark on the driving course; I just wanted to get through and pass. As usual I didn't have the self-belief to envisage otherwise.

Despite the rigours of the job, it fitted me like a glove. I had few regrets about joining the Met and looked forward optimistically. There was one thing I wanted to change, however, and that was where I lived. I didn't like the ugly sixties block that is Tottenham section house; although I had my own room and shared facilities, I found it institutional. As much as anything else, though, I didn't like the area — I couldn't shake off the memories of the riots and the feeling of trepidation they had instilled in me as a young police cadet — so I was delighted when I moved to the expensive elegance of Highgate, and the red-brick

Edwardian section house on the hill. The police owned the building, intended to accommodate single officers, though they have since sold it. I lived rent-free, thereby forfeiting any rent allowance in my salary. I was happy there, and although the storm of 1987 rattled the windows of the house mercilessly, they withstood the assault, which was more than I could the rising tide of my independence. In early 1988 I moved into a small studio flat I'd bought in Chingford, Essex. This was my first attempt at living on my own, and it felt marvellous.

On a personal level things were going well for me. I had started to see Pat Kelly. I liked him very much, though I wanted to keep things casual. Before him, I had been on an occasional date, usually with a colleague, but being new to London and the Met, I had been happy to concentrate on my career and finding my way around. I liked living on my own, coming and going from work, pleasing myself. I wasn't really interested in meeting anyone. I didn't want to get too involved. I was young and in my prime, and I enjoyed my life the way it was.

CHAPTER 4

MARRIAGE, MOTHERHOOD AND NOT HAVING IT ALL

I was a WPC who was going places. Others had gone before me, but it hadn't been until 1919 that a hundred women police patrols and women sergeants were appointed to the Met, albeit at first only on a temporary basis. As the First World War swallowed up the men, so women emerged in the workplace. Although the WPCs' arrival was met initially with suspicion and hostility, by 1923 the Home Secretary agreed that twenty female officers could be retained, and in that April they were sworn in as constables. Their role was essentially protective and preventive. In those days WPCs patrolled streets and parks but were later ruled out of even the most mundane aspects of police work, such as riding a motorbike or dog-handling. It was 1974 before WPCs were given equal pay and the same training, duties and opportunities for promotion as men.

When WPC Agnes Thornton joined the Met's Paddington Green station in 1925 her duties were limited to working with children and women in a family context, or with low-key postings such as guarding at-risk women in hospitals. Many serving male chief constables felt that even that sort of work should be dealt with by voluntary organisations and could see no role alongside them for women. Joining any special-operations group, as I did in 1994 with SO19, the Firearms Unit, would have been out of the question. In any case, WPCs were not admitted to that until 1991. Even by the last decade of the twentieth century women didn't have access to all levels of the police service.

In 1990, Alison Halford, then assistant chief constable of Merseyside and Britain's top-ranking woman police officer, had reached a very high position in a very male world. She'd swept ahead at a majestic rate — until she decided she wanted to go one rank higher and found that she couldn't. She had become frustrated when she applied for promotion nine times and nine times was rejected. In the end she took her employers to the Equal Opportunities Commission and said she'd been sexually discriminated against. Her action triggered a fierce smear campaign by the police; she found herself suspended on full pay, a litany of misdemeanours invoked in support of their response. Technically the case ended in a draw, when in 1992 Halford agreed to drop her charges if the police dropped theirs. She received £140,000 in compensation and a yearly pension of £35,000. But the moral victory might be seen as hers when in 1997 the European Court of Human Rights upheld her complaint that the police had invaded her privacy by tapping her phones during the campaign by both sides to prove their case.

At the turn of the century all this would have been unthinkable, but within the context of what was available to her then Agnes Thornton did well. Records from a hearing at Marylebone Magistrates' Court describe her as bold for successfully taking on a drunk and disorderly labourer on the Edgware Road. He was fined fifteen shillings. However, it was not only WPC Thornton's duties that were restricted but also her working day, which was confined to the hours between eight in the morning and midnight. What would she have made of the shift work that I did as a matter of course? What's more, there was none of the new technology that we all now take for granted. Her only means of calling for rapid-response back-up was to blow hard on a whistle.

Agnes Thornton would never have made the progression from walker to driver, because patrolling was done only on foot, often alone, or by public transport. Although when I started at Hornsey we were encouraged to use public transport, to hop on the bus or take the tube, presumably WPC Thornton didn't follow my course of action when, in pursuit of a burglar, I flagged down a passing car. By the time it had stopped, I'd explained and climbed in, my colleagues had made the arrest a few hundred yards further down the road. And when it came to moving fast Agnes Thornton wasn't only slowed up by having to walk her beat. Her uniform, a long, thick skirt with a jacket belted at the waist, must have inhibited her. And though the calf-length lace-up leather boots might have been good for running in, the regulation wide-brimmed hat would have been more of a hindrance than a help: it would have needed a hand on it to stop it flying off when she was moving at speed.

I read about Agnes Thornton in the Met's the *Job*. There was a short interview with her as she approached her hundreth birthday in the mid-1990s. She claimed that Londoners had been more law-abiding in the twenties, with muggings and drugs almost non-existent. She also felt she had been spoiled by her male colleagues, her worst experience the occasion when they had decided to use her hat as a dartboard. I wish! She remained in the service until she married a fellow PC in 1927. In my experience this was the fate of a large number of female officers. Once they got married and had children, they left the service. Once it happened to me I could understand why: the shift work alone was a huge deterrent, never mind everything else. But I can be stubborn, and the tougher things get, the more I dig in my heels and refuse to budge. I was determined to pursue my career. When things changed radically for me, not so long after that first date with Pat, I was adamant that my life would stay the same. Some hope!

Our relationship had started in a low-key way. He was in the same division and relief as me, which meant that we worked the same shifts; I was based at Hornsey, and he at Wood Green. I knew him as a colleague, and I was aware that he'd got married not long after my arrival in February 1986. I remember him bringing in the baby pictures nine months later, and hearing soon after that he and his wife, Donna, were separating.

Pat's family is Irish, although he was born and brought up in Edmonton, north London. I liked him: he was just one of the lads, a bit of a practical joker at work, quite loud and boisterous. After his break with Donna, we began to go around together, out for the occasional drink at one or other of the favourite pubs on the ground: the Shepherd in Highgate, the Alex in Muswell Hill. We also went training, at the Tower, a bodybuilding gym in Church Street, Edmonton. With a colleague from Hornsey, Pat was into serious bodybuilding at a competitive level. I used to train with them on the men's side of the gym, but I wasn't interested in competing. Nevertheless I was, and still am, pretty strong. I had something of a reputation for being so. It led to some funny moments sometimes, such as the time DI Jones summoned me into his office. It must be said that I thought he was as mad as a hatter anyway, so when he proceeded to strip off to the waist, saying, 'Now, Helen, would you please show me how to do sit-ups,' I wasn't the least surprised or alarmed. He'd been on a diet and had lost a lot of weight, and was now engaged in a fitness campaign. I duly turned the floor of his office into a temporary gymnasium.

It was admirable of him, really, because once you leave Hendon, there's no compulsion to keep fit. Also, once you graduate from being a walker to being a driver, as I just had, you don't even get the exercise that foot patrol offers. The shift system doesn't make things any easier, perpetuating an unhealthy lifestyle, encouraging bad eating habits and fragmenting your sleep pattern. But to my mind the job requires a certain standard of fitness, and I feel there should be some kind of regular fitness test, related to your age. Many were the times when I would find myself running down the road after somebody and needing all my lung and muscle power to keep going. And a year or two later I know that it was my rock-hard abdominal muscles that protected my internal organs from a vicious attack. Perhaps I was lucky too, but I'm sure this was part of my luck.

Despite the antisocial nature of our work, Pat and I slowly got to know each other. On our first proper date we went to a pub called the Owl in Lippitts Hill, directly opposite Lippitts Hill Training Camp, where the SO19 Firearms Unit is based. This was somewhere that would figure large in my life in years to come, as for now Pat was about to do. Within two years we had married and had a child. Once I've decided to do something I don't waste time. In this instance I should have looked before I leapt.

Pat had moved out of his parents' house and bought a flat in Cheshunt with a friend. It was right at the peak of the property boom, around 1988, and they paid an extortionate amount of money for a two-bedroom apartment, which left him eventually with huge negative equity. In a sort of musical chairs, I sold my flat and moved in with him at the beginning of 1989, while his flatmate moved out to be with his girlfriend. Our living together was no problem at work and no one batted an eyelid: even though we were both on B-Relief, we didn't overlap professionally. At home, though, the problems were not slow in starting. We were both going through the same stresses and strains of shift work, both tired at the same time. Now when my husband Steve, also a police officer, is exhausted from early turn, I'm not. It's a great help. Otherwise it's a recipe for an argument: you both want to let off steam and you can't because neither of you is prepared really to listen to the other.

Around 1989 interest rates soared, and we found ourselves with monthly mortgage repayments of £1,000, which instantly swallowed one of our wage packets. It was ridiculous, and it didn't do us any favours: it's well known that one of the things couples argue about most is money. We were no exception. Plus I had the feeling that we were trapped in that flat for ever because the property market nose-dived: house prices plummeted, interest rates were sky high, which made it difficult for us to move on even if we'd planned it.

Pat had the complication that he was getting a divorce, so he had an ex-wife and a young child to consider as well as me. This wasn't an easy time: all of a sudden I'd gone from being single and independent to having a complicated life. It was a mammoth change. Pat is an extremely nice man and very kind. From the start he did all the shopping, looked after our finances and generally took the greatest care of me. But he was almost too nice, and I soon began to feel my personality smothered by the relationship. Looking back, I realise that our relationship should have stayed on the dating level then fizzled out naturally. But it developed a momentum of its own. I'm not sure that I was ready to get married, but Pat was the marrying kind. Some people are like that. They like to be married. I was only twenty-three, and I'd never been married. Pat was six years older than me, and he had, and he liked the married state. I had feelings for Pat, and I went along with them, but I had reservations too, even at the time, which were soon sidelined when I discovered I was pregnant. We brought forward the date of our wedding from June to April 1990.

I had the works: a beautiful white dress with a pony and trap to take me to the church. We stood under the apple trees in the orchard of my parents' house in Childswickham for our photos. The sun shone on a lovely day in early summer. It was idyllic, the ceremony conducted in the pretty village church, the catered reception in the village hall with all our family and friends around us. We had a few days' honeymoon in Italy, then went back to work.

By now I had moved stations from Hornsey to Muswell Hill. This is a less urban part of London with the huge green space of Alexandra Palace and a lower crime rate. I was still training every day, in the gym at the local sports centre in Cheshunt, or out running. Later in my pregnancy I modified my regime so that I no longer lifted the massive weights I had been using and in the final stage I started swimming. When I had found out I was pregnant, my relief inspector, Trevor Taylor, put me on office-based duties, helping out where I was needed, no longer out on the street and dealing with the public, which was considered potentially dangerous for me in my condition. Light duties were standard on all divisions for pregnant beat officers. I helped out with the warrants, sorting out the files of the people who were on the division's wanted list.

Of the thirty members of our relief, five were women. I was one of the first women on the division to have a baby then return to work. Historically, most women had left the service. At that point I can't think of any other WPC in the Met who had a baby. None of the other women on any of the Hornsey reliefs had children at that stage, so in that sense I was completely on my own. I had no role models, no one with whom to compare notes, and no one to talk to about what I might expect once I came back to work in my changed family circumstances.

Ben's arrival signalled the second big change in my life. Everyone told me it would, though I was determined to believe otherwise. It wasn't that I didn't adore Ben, and I had wanted children, though perhaps not immediately. He was born on 1 November 1990 at Chase Farm Hospital, Enfield. In a bizarre twist of fate this was the very hospital to which I was taken later, when I was shot. Ben was two weeks overdue, so he had been induced. He weighed 6lb 10oz and arrived at about four in the afternoon via a forceps delivery because he was in some distress. Apart from family, friends from work came to visit and brought us flowers, cards and presents. I did not take him in to the station before I returned to work: a police station is not the right place for a baby. Some might argue that neither is it for a woman with children, but obviously I wouldn't agree with that — although later I realised the tremendous strain the nature of the job imposes on you when you have a young child to consider.

I had four months' maternity leave, during which time we got a cat, Chloe, a gorgeous short-haired British Blue with a wonderful temperament, ideally suited to a family with a young baby. As a child I had always had a cat, and I felt the time had come to get one. My domestic situation was firming up, but not so much that I wasn't averse to returning to work in February 1991, back to the full shifts I had done before I knew I was pregnant. Pat had taken a nine-to-five job as a crime prevention officer (CPO). He had regular hours with weekends off. Looking back I realise this was very good of him, because he accommodated my career, which a lot of men wouldn't. CPO wasn't a job that he really wanted to do: he was doing it simply because it would fit in with us, so that Ben wasn't spending too long with a child-minder and I could carry on with shift work.

Our first child-minder was the wife of a colleague, but she had never done any child-minding before and she didn't really take to it. While I was still with Pat we juggled our work patterns. Later, when I was on my own, I had to get a full-time nanny, Michelle, who travelled to my house and covered all the shifts, even those that started at five in the morning. I went through lots of different nannies over the years. At that time, though, depending on which shift I was doing, Pat would drop off Ben and I would pick him up, or the other way round. Quite often Ben wasn't away from us for long because our shifts overlapped. If, for example, I was on late turn and Pat was doing nine to five, he would only be apart from us for three or four hours. We had an even bigger financial burden, though, with child-minding costs added to our steadily rising mortgage.

If I had been so inclined, I suppose I could have got an office-bound job on the divisional crime desk, although openings for these are limited. But I just wasn't the type. It wasn't me. I didn't want that. The thought of being in an office was abhorrent to me. My career, despite my marriage and Ben's arrival, was still important to me. It was my choice to go back and carry on as I had before. It was tiring, but I was determined. I remember sitting at home before a nightshift, and some nights feeling absolutely exhausted, even before my shift began. But I wanted to keep up with the men, to pull my weight along with the rest, with no allowances made. I was determined not to be any different just because I had become a mum. So, whatever it took, all the juggling of priorities, the strain on my marriage and within the family, the different child-minders and nannies for Ben, the personal side of my life had to fit into my work. It was a precarious balancing act. But I wanted it all.

Adapting to shift work again was hard after having been away from it for nearly a year. During each shift there were supposed to be forty-five-minute rest periods, but often these were absorbed into the day, especially if a call came when you simply got up and left. You could eat in the canteen, where the early turns would have breakfast at either 9 a.m. or 10 a.m.; sometimes there was no rest until noon, although if it was quiet you might get an hour. You had to play it by ear, not by the book. In the afternoon your rest was around five or six o'clock, and on nights you took your break when you could, usually around one or two, when quite often you would stay out in the Panda and eat a sandwich, watching the cars go by. The shift system has all changed now with sector policing. The four reliefs per station became six teams; the idea was to have extra people on at busier times, such as 4 p.m. to midnight on a Friday night. In principle it's a good idea, but in practice everyone knew it wouldn't work because there weren't enough officers to make up four shifts, never mind six teams. In some divisions they have now reduced the six to five, and I think there's a move back to the original four.

There's been a lot of change since I joined the Met in 1985. Recruitment is down, and the starting wage at Hendon is now around £700 a month, which is not nearly as good as I got in the mid-eighties. Wages and allowances have been cut: there's no rent allowance, no tokens any more to get your uniform dry-cleaned, no dental costs paid. At Hendon Police Training School you now have to pay for your room; if you live in a section house you have to pay rent; you have to pay to live in police flats. All of that was free when I started out. In 1993 the report of the Sheehy Inquiry into Police Responsibilities and Rewards, which related to the force and its efficiency — which was quite radical and, I think, quite outrageous in many of its suggestions — was presented to the Home Secretary. It provided a means by which assessment of pay within the formula established by the Edmund Davies Committee, appointed in 1977 to review the machinery for negotiating police pay following a period of discontent, was broken. The then Labour government had appointed the committee of inquiry that recommended this formula by which future pay settlements could be established: in the 1970s many police officers were on the breadline. Some felt it necessary to demand the right to strike in order to press claims that would otherwise be ignored. The poor levels of pay had led to corruption and general dissatisfaction. The committee of inquiry came up with a new financial package and ensured that police officers received a living wage. From then on wages were reasonably good, but the Edmund Davies agreement has been dropped. Although New Labour said they weren't going to institute the changes suggested by the

Sheehy Report, in fact, they've gradually brought in different aspects of it, in my view compounding the damage to the force already done by the Tories. The Conservative government under John Major started to introduce the Sheehy changes, which Labour is continuing. It seems to me that we'll end up back where we were in the early 1970s. Money is not the prime motivating factor in working for the police service, but wages have to be good enough to attract a certain standard of person. You're not supposed to have another job as well, but some people can't survive without one. I know of one police officer who was entitled to income support but never claimed it because he was too proud, and others who do bits of work such as painting and decorating or window cleaning on the side. But that shouldn't happen because police work is demanding and everyone needs their time off. When I joined in the mid-1980s it wasn't like that.

The changes that I underwent in 1990 were entirely personal, though. When I was single and before Ben came along, I would sometimes go out after work with my relief. I remember going to Smithfield market at 6.30 a.m. for breakfast, followed by the pub before going home in the afternoon to sleep before the night shift. I only did that once! Now my opportunities for fun were restricted — no, that kind of thing was just an impossibility. I couldn't even go home and go to bed as I normally would. After an early turn, for example, when I finished at two in the afternoon, I might be feeling like a mid-afternoon nap. But not with a baby around. If I'd been on early turn, then I'd have been able to pick up Ben from the child-minder's around 2.30 p.m. and take him home. Then I had him to look after and a training session to fit in. Pat would arrive back between

5.30 and 6 p.m., so he would help. I was very driven, but it was exhausting, and I'd frequently be asleep on the settee by eight o'clock in the evening. Fortunately I was lucky with Ben, who, right from the word go, had an easy-going personality. My life would have been much harder had he not been such a laid-back little boy, who appeared mostly to take everything in his stride. When I think back over the number of child-minders and nannies to whom he had to adapt, I cringe. But I really had no choice because I had no extended family support. There was nobody except Pat and me. Occasionally we would collect Pat's mother from Edmonton to babysit, but neither she nor his father were really in a position to help us. Both of them worked full time, so they didn't have much time to spare.

Pat was obsessive about bodybuilding and, as a consequence, fussy about what he would and would not eat. He would never indulge himself with a biscuit or a slice of cake with his cup of tea; he was very strict with himself. He may have changed now, but at that stage, when he was coming up to a bodybuilding competition, he would only eat rice, chicken and vegetables and only drink water. That was it. He would diet so that all the fat came off his muscles, so they showed up better. As the competition drew closer he would only drink water and eat rice. This went on for months. He used sun-beds, and shaved the whole of his body. It took over his life and had an effect on his personality. Before we married I didn't know him very well, because we hadn't been together very long, but the strict regime that goes with bodybuilding can make people tunnel-visioned with little time or patience for anything else.

I wasn't a particularly easy person to live with because I

was so independent. I had been used to living on my own, and I like my own space, which is one thing you don't have much of when you're living with someone, you have a new baby and you're doing full-time shift work. I was no saint at all: I could be bad-tempered with the best of them. We were both under pressure.

So what do I always do when I find myself overstressed? Take on more, of course. It's my way of proving to myself that I can cope, I guess. In May 1991, with Pat's agreement, I applied to join the Territorial Support Group (TSG), a unit trained to deal with public-order events and riots, with anything potentially violent, be it a mentally ill person or a protest march. Pat had belonged to it back in the mid-eighties when he had been posted to Broadwater Farm. With hindsight, I realise this might have been the straw that broke the camel's back, and I must have been a bit mad to think I could take it on. Apart from anything else, the duty times were inconsistent and demanding, but I was blinkered by the single-mindedness of my ambition. I studied hard for a board interview, and on the day of the oral examination I was questioned for about forty-five minutes on the law, police procedure, the TSG and current affairs. A few days later I heard that I had come top at the assessment and interview, which pleased me greatly. Pat was totally behind me when I confirmed that I would join the TSG later that year. But, as events were to unfold, I never did.

I can't quite remember when the cracks in our relationship began to show. But I do know that Barry Murphy played a part in the equation that was eventually to equal divorce. PS 87YR Barry Murphy arrived at Hornsey Division as a newly qualified sergeant in the midsummer of 1991. I was very much into work, which was by then the lynchpin of my existence, and I was very much into Barry: we clicked right from the beginning. I was a bit flirtatious with him when he first joined the division, but nothing more. I thought he was great, and the feeling was mutual. But I was married, and I had a child. I didn't know much about Barry's personal life except that early on he revealed that he was to be married in six weeks. What I did know was that every time I saw him I got butterflies in my stomach.

He's the sort you either love or hate on first meeting, but once you get to know him you realise there's a lot more to him. He is what I consider a typical Cancerian: quiet and sensitive on the inside, but the exterior can convey the exact opposite. Because he's so sensitive, Barry can be difficult, moody and complicated. No one's perfect, though when we became emotionally entangled this was something about him that I found difficult. Then I was so bound up in my own needs and couldn't cope with anything more than what was happening to me, and I think he felt that I couldn't give him the support he needed. I was take, take, take, all the time on an emotional level. I needed him to support me. When I was no longer with Pat, and Barry and I were half living together, there was no space to deal with this as there had been when we only saw one another at work.

Barry could be abrupt and forthright in his dealings with others, and he sometimes appears brash, but I never found this a problem. He seemed to care deeply about people, which I find quite unusual in a man, and everyone at Hornsey knew that if they had a problem they could go to Barry. He would always make time to listen and help if he could. He was very appreciative of anyone who was good at what they did, whether they were male or female, and as someone in a position of authority he was a firm believer in equal opportunities.

As a new sergeant at Hornsey, Barry was driven to make the best of himself. He admired me professionally, and he told me so. Despite evidence to the contrary, I had never thought I was good at my job, and he reassured me continually. I found him tremendously encouraging. Apart from this, Barry was the first man I'd ever looked at and thought, Wow! In fact, he bowled me over. The effect he had on me was like a thunderbolt. The first time I saw him, I remember so well the extraordinary impact he made on me, and it was not just because I found him incredibly handsome, the original tall, dark version. We have spoken about it often, and Barry believes that he was meant to be there to help me during that period of my life. In some way I feel that maybe he was my guardian angel at that time.

There was an incredibly powerful connection between us. The first time I heard his name I felt it, when someone was talking about him as the new sergeant. He had come second out of all the Met officers who had passed the sergeants' exams that year and was to be posted from Holloway, another north London station, to Hornsey. Even his name stuck in my mind: Barry Murphy. He had been born in Wood Green and, like Pat, is of Irish parentage. His father had died when he was four, and his mother had brought up the family on her own. I didn't know much more than that about him.

To become a sergeant Barry had taken a written exam. The next step up was to become an inspector, for which there were written and oral examinations. After this you are interviewed for the position of chief inspector, chief superintendent (a position that existed in my day but has now been phased out), commander, deputy assistant commissioner, assistant commissioner and then commissioner. Only a few women have made commander and deputy assistant commissioner. The current Metropolitan Police commissioner, Paul Condon, isn't very popular for all sorts of reasons, but many Met officers dislike the tenure policy he introduced, which makes it impossible to stay in a post for more than five years. This is disruptive in all sorts of ways. He also tends to harp on about the service's negative points whenever he appears on the news; he never seems to back the police, to stand up for his own. I think this is how he is seen, as something of a yes-man to all the politicians and media, all those who complain about the police. I am not saying that there aren't bad elements in the Met, both human and operational, because there are. But the majority of Met officers are very good, and the work they do is fantastic. Most people, the general public included, just don't know about the risks some officers take every day of their working lives. It's a dirty job in part, and someone's got to do it. I believe that Paul Condon could do more for the police by pointing this out. He could achieve a better balance.

When Barry first started on Hornsey Division he was based at Hornsey police station and worked on my relief. I was by then at Wood Green, and I told him that he should come to work with us because I thought he would find the work more interesting. Before too long he switched stations. One of his duties as sergeant was to take parades at the start of a shift. If it was early turn, B-Relief would all get together, at 6 a.m. in the morning in a little room in the station. Barry, or the sergeant on duty, would read from the parade book any information he felt it vital that the new relief should know. You would then be allocated your postings for the day, driving the van or walking 1A beat, and you'd be given your 'refs' times, when in theory you could take your break for refreshment. Parades were once an important part of the day, originally the point when you would have shown all your 'appointments' — your whistle, notebook, truncheon — for inspection. As the years have gone by, this has become a less formal occasion, until it distilled to the postings session we had then. Once he was ensconced at Wood Green, Barry would quite often post himself with me. I suppose that, strictly speaking, this isn't particularly professional, but there was no harm in it.

After you were posted, you would go to pick up the logbook for the car or van that you were driving, in which were kept the keys for the vehicle, plus a record of the mileage and accident damage. Then you'd go and have a cup of tea, unless it was busy and you got straight out. That time working with Barry at Wood Green was among the best times I had with the Met. We always had fun. The relief was good, and by then I was one of the senior PCs on it. This was when the joke developed about my popularity with the public on the streets — How many times is she going to be asked out today? Whenever I came in for tea or coffee, the colleague I'd been out with on patrol used to announce the day's tally. I found it really amusing.

Early one summer morning, around 2 a.m. we all went up to Alexandra Palace to play football. Unusually for me, I wasn't involved in the game, but I watched keenly from the edge. At one point the ball was kicked over a wire fence that surrounded some renovation work under way in the grounds. One of the PCs climbed over the fence to retrieve it and became entangled in the wire netting on his way back. The metal buttons of his jacket got caught in the fence hoops and they tore off one by one as he descended, each one ripping off with a wonderful ping. I have a store of images like these that remind me of the tremendous feeling of camaraderie that existed then.

When Barry and I were posted out together we would chat all night between calls. I would talk about how things were at home, and he was a good listener, good at giving advice. I suppose that summer of 1991 my fate was sealed. Getting on so well with Barry made me even more aware of the dissatisfaction I felt in my marriage. I couldn't talk to Pat. Although he was quite loud and jovial at work, at home he was always quiet, not a communicator. A lot of it was my fault in that, although I cared about him, I had little knowledge of relationships before I met him and our marriage was my first proper experience of one. I had nothing and no one with whom to compare him. I guess I behaved selfishly because I loved my job, and as that was of paramount importance to me perhaps I didn't put enough into our life together.

The time after my return to the Met after Ben's birth was great at work — partly because I could see Barry, partly because I could focus on my police work — but I wasn't happy at home. Home was relegated to the back burner. The flat in Cheshunt was very bare, in part because all my energy went into work and juggling my time to accommodate it. I didn't make any time for my home. There were few ornaments or pictures and although it was always clean, it was never homely. I never really made a home with Pat. I didn't want to be married. Apart from

Ben, who was wonderful, I didn't want to be there. My heart was in my work, where I was almost always on a high, working obsessively and never frightened to get stuck into whatever it threw at me. Now that Barry Murphy had arrived there was no hope for a future with Pat, no matter how much I might have wanted it to be otherwise.

Barry had his own preoccupations. It wasn't long before I discovered that he had called off his wedding. He is a man of strong principles, quite unusual these days, I find. Cancelling his marriage plans was a complicated decision for him, and I don't know the ins and outs of it. I do know that part of the reason was that he decided he could not go through with it when he felt as he did about me. I was later to discover that commitment frightens him, though no doubt one day he will meet the right person.

The way I felt about Barry was too important and meaningful to ignore, even though it meant separating from Ben's father. Ours was a relationship of equals on every level, not only physically and emotionally but also spiritually. We had so much in common. Tall and well built, Barry is, like me, into training. He enjoys working out in the gym, but running is his passion. Sometimes, if it was quiet on nights, we would go for a run on a circuit that took us around the empty, echoing streets of Wood Green. This is what we were doing one night at the beginning of September, along with a couple of the other officers. They dropped out after a bit, and Barry and I went further on our own. I remember him saying to me that I was the first woman with whom he had trained who had ever been able to keep up with him. That pleased me. I was very attracted to him in so many ways, and part of it was how much he admired me. Sometimes I think, though, that I fell in love with the image of Barry Murphy, Sergeant as Hero, as he fell for Helen Kelly — as I was then called — Superwoman PC, dynamic, fit and active, always arresting people. We loved these aspects of each other. But there is more than one side to everyone. As we would later discover.

For now it was a mutual-admiration society. And in many ways I'd never felt so good. When we got back from our run that night I even let myself indulge in a delicious meal that Jeni Lawson, one of the other WPCs on my relief, had prepared. I had been dieting for a while, and I had lost quite a lot of weight, but I just couldn't resist: Jeni is a very good cook. At three in the morning we tucked into a wonderfully spicy chilli con carne followed by the juiciest summer pudding. If only I'd known it was almost my last supper.

CHAPTER 5

THE STABBING: CARELESS IN THE COMMUNITY

We used to call it Mad Monday, and that particular Monday, 2 September 1991, was no exception. On any other quick-changeover day, with only eight hours between shifts, there was no time for anything, and certainly none to celebrate the sixth anniversary of the start of my career in the Met. I got to bed shortly after 6 a.m. and was up again for the afternoon shift at two. I hadn't had much rest. While I slept Pat had taken Ben to the child-minder. I wasn't due to see him at all that day, because his dad would pick him up at five and give him his tea before bed. I just concentrated on getting through the shift ahead when I awoke around noon. Unusually for me I ate two bowls of Ready Brek before I left the house at 1 p.m. I would be thankful for that later.

It was very hot for early September. At the station I put on my uniform and went straight on parade, taken that shift by Sergeant John Davison, 26YR, sector sergeant for the day. I was to drive the van, Yankee Delta 2. Just as we were about to disperse, unusually for him, John broke into *Hill Street Blues*' speak, his last, prophetic words to us, 'And let's be careful out there.'

I logged what he said, but I was thinking about other things, such as my disappointment that Barry would not be coming out with me as my operator. At the last minute, as custody sergeant that Monday, he had a bail case to handle, a police officer who had been arrested on a drink-drive offence. In his place John was to be my passenger. Sarge, as I knew him, was a lovely bloke, also into training, and we got on well.

After parade we had a quick cup of tea, collected the keys to the van and the logbook, and booked out a radio from the store in the front office. Quite often the radios didn't work properly, and there were areas in which they didn't receive or transmit at all: black spots, where you were out of contact with the control room. The radio system was antiquated and needed updating. It was eventually but, like the Met's new computer system, it's still not state-of-the-art. A dodgy radio was a bit of a drawback, though some people think that radios have taken the invention out of police work. In the old days you had to walk your beat, get out and about, and meet people. You had to learn to talk your way out of trouble. Now all you did was shout for assistance on the PR.

Knowing that all the Met's radios could be linked through the Incident Room (IR) at Scotland Yard, I found mine reassuring. With any major incident that required urgent assistance the controller at Hornsey Division could go through on the computer to the Yard and ask for a link. Once this was in place any officer on the main set, the fixed radio in every vehicle, could hear everyone else, though in those days you couldn't link the PRs. I was glad of my radio, and later I'd be more than grateful for the call sign Urgent Assistance.

Though I felt disappointed that it wasn't Barry beside me as I clipped on my PR and climbed into the van, I knew John was a good stand-in. As we left the yard at Wood Green I was feeling well below par from lack of sleep, and my eyes were burning, but we had an eight-hour shift ahead so there was no point in grumbling. With my notebook and a pen in my pocket, and a few fond memories in my head, we began our patrol around the streets of north London on the lookout as normal. It was six years ago that I'd started out as a new recruit at Hendon. A lot had happened since.

There was another anniversary that September, and as it

seemed quiet I asked John if he'd mind if I went to order Nana some flowers. Her birthday was in two days' time. I had just jumped back in the van when the fateful call came over the PR. It was approaching four o'clock, an hour away from rush-hour. A man — six-foot plus, well-built, black — was causing a disturbance in Paradise, a clothes shop in Wood Green High Road. This was an everyday call, nothing out of the ordinary, and the only reason we accepted it was because there was nothing more important to distract us.

We were making our way there with no great urgency when I spotted two of the other WPCs from B-Relief in a Panda. Jeni Lawson and Zara Kingdom had accepted the call originally, and we were there as back-up, but in the spirit of fun I decided I'd get there first. I speeded up and pulled out into the High Road. This late turn had proved such an uneventful shift that a little one-upmanship with my colleagues would brighten up the day. There we were, John and I, just happy to be in front of the others, and to amuse ourselves still further we started the usual playful banter.

'Hope you've got your handcuffs, maybe there'll be a fight.'

'Yeah, I've got them. We'll be all right.'

It was a busy Monday afternoon on Wood Green High Road, and hordes of shoppers were milling about when we drew up alongside the kerb outside Paradise. From the description we'd been given of the suspect it was quite easy to identify him amid the throng of street activity: a gigantic West Indian man dressed in a black anorak and orange trousers with a strange, staring look to his eyes. We had taken off our jackets, it was shirtsleeves weather, and there he stood dressed in a heavy jacket, ranting on the pavement outside the shop. That he was our man was soon confirmed by his lumbering departure across the road as soon as he saw us arrive. I jumped out of the van and followed him through the heavy afternoon traffic, dodging the cars and buses. John headed off to Paradise to have a word with the informants.

The suspect, all fourteen stone of him, stopped on the footpath on the other side of the street near a pedestrian precinct lined with market stalls. He parked himself in front of the vast complex of the Wood Green Shopping City. Jeni and Zara were hard on my heels, but I wanted to be the one to approach and talk to him first. I was still a keen PC, even after six years' service. My arrest levels in the previous months had been high; it had almost become a game. I played to win.

'Hello. May I have a word, please?' He stood with his huge back to me as I uttered the usual introductory platitudes. When he reacted to my question as if an electric charge had bolted through his body I knew at once that something was wrong in a very major way. Sure enough, when he turned round sharply it was to take a swing at me. With a punch to my stomach so powerful that it knocked the wind out of me I went flying — all five foot ten and eleven stone of me that, at that time, was mostly muscle.

I landed on the pavement some twelve feet away. As I picked myself up I was aware of an excruciating pain in my stomach. But I felt too angry to be scared or distracted by it. With my left hand gripping where it hurt, I struggled quickly to my feet. Teeth gritted, I went back to tackle him. Did he really think he could punch me and get away with it? With my right hand I grabbed my PR, locating the mouthpiece, which had gone AWOL on its extendable cable, and punched the buttons frantically to call for urgent assistance. I rushed back towards my assailant and caught a split-second vision of Jeni stumbling off-balance and flying past me to my right. Without missing a beat I was floored by another almighty punch that propelled me backwards from where I'd come and left me sprawling several feet away on the pavement.

It was becoming more than tedious, but when I tried to get up this time I couldn't. A fountain of blood gushed from me, turning my crisp white shirt a bright, damp sticky scarlet. As I watched in disbelief, all I could think was, God, he's punched me so hard I'm bleeding. All around me I was aware of people screaming, and to my right somewhere dimly I saw John approach the suspect. I couldn't raise myself. I slumped down and cradled the arm from which the blood was pumping out of me. It wouldn't stop and flowed down my front and into my lap like a river in flood. I began to shake. All of a sudden I felt panic-stricken and very afraid. A couple of women who'd been out shopping peeled off from the crowd that had gathered and began to give me first aid. They made me up a makeshift bed on the pavement, and as I lay there one took my arm and held it high in the air above my head. I tried to speak into my PR to request an ambulance, but everything started to blur.

Zara was only twenty, and still a probationer, but she was a godsend to me at that moment. Hers were the most welcome words I could have hoped to hear: 'Helen needs an ambulance.'

It was only as I lay on that pavement that I realised what had happened to me. 'My God,' said one of the women who was tending me, 'she's been stabbed in the stomach too!' It wasn't until I heard this that I knew my assailant had been in possession of a knife. It had never entered my head. I never even saw it. But Rupert West, as we subsequently knew him to be, a thirty-seven-year-old Jamaican-born man who had come to Britain in 1964, had held a Swiss Army knife clenched tight in his fist. He had a string of convictions going back to 1974, interspersed with periods in psychiatric institutions that had started in 1972. And at that moment he also had the longest blade of his knife poking out between his fingers. This had turned his punch into a lethal weapon. With it, in less than a minute that autumn afternoon, he had stabbed us four attending officers a total of ten times. He knifed me once in the stomach and twice in my left arm. Jeni had five stab wounds on and around her upper chest. Zara was knifed in the arm, and John in the stomach. He caused all this human damage until such time as John and off-duty PC Peter Crawford managed to talk him down from his killing frenzy and persuade him to surrender the knife.

By the time West was arrested, virtually every police officer in the vicinity had turned up. Ian Craven, a dog handler who was to become a neighbour, had accepted the call. He remembers the chaos that ensued when all the rush-hour traffic came to a standstill in that area of north London. Oddly, Steve, who is now my husband, had been on his way too, as part of the ARV unit to which he then belonged. The Trojan car for the Wood Green area was refused permission to run by the IR, but Steve's car carried on because they knew that officers at the scene were injured. On that occasion we never met because the slow-moving traffic made sure that he didn't get there before I'd left. This was all quite a coincidence, given the major role that Steve has gone on to play in my life and happiness. But what happened to me on the Wood Green High Road that

warm anniversary day had other, less welcome reper-
cussions for me. Though I did not know it then, that day
changed my life for ever.

A massive crowd had gathered around us: the usual mix
of the actively concerned and the idly curious mingled with
those who had a genuine reason to be there. One woman
stepped over the police tape and headed towards the back
of an ambulance from which she emerged with a bottle
of smelling-salts. These she waved under the nose of
John Davison. Some bystanders were more malevolent,
dismissing us with a callous, 'You've got what you deserve.'
The crowd picked up and ran with the jeer, repeating it in a
malicious, swelling refrain. Though in the Wood Green
community there was a lot of anti-police sentiment, it was
pure spite. One woman was arrested for shouting, 'I hope
they die.'

And there was more, just as bad, if not worse. While
John lay on the pavement PC Crawford's girlfriend was
kneeling beside him, giving him first aid. She had her hands
over the stab wound, applying pressure in an attempt to
stem the bleeding. He was seriously hurt, almost
disembowelled, as prosecutor John Bevan put it during
West's trial the following year at the Old Bailey. A group of
youths approached, and one crouched down beside her. He
pulled away her hands and said, 'Let's see if he's done him
good.' She told them forcefully to fuck off. It was an order
she delivered with such ferocity and venom that they
obeyed it immediately.

This was just about as disgusting as it could get, and the
papers were full of it later after the trial. 'Stab Cops
Taunted By Crowd' was how the *Sun* phrased it, while
Today ran the headline 'Knifed WPCs Jeered At By

Shoppers'. Thankfully I didn't hear any of it. Neither was I aware that some of the crowd were arrested that day for their threatening behaviour and for the things they were saying. Later in court, though, all cases against them were dismissed, including that of the woman who, it was alleged, had hoped we would die. For unlawful detention, she was awarded a sum far in excess of the amount that any of we police casualties received from the Criminal Injuries Compensation Board.

Because of the appalling traffic, several police officers abandoned their vehicles and made their way to us on foot. Among them may have been PC Angus Naismith, because he was the first PC to my rescue. It was wonderful to see a friendly face, and all I could think was, Thank God, I'm safe. While Angus knelt above me, I held on to his ankles like someone drowning at sea might cling to a piece of driftwood. 'You'll be OK, Helen. It'll be all right,' he reassured me repeatedly. What he was saying sounded to me then like the most fantastic words I had ever heard in my life. I never did thank him enough for the comfort he brought me or tell him how much he helped me at that dreadful moment. Don't die, don't die, I kept telling myself. I knew that I had to stay awake and in control. I didn't want to become unconscious. I had to keep on breathing. Don't die. Don't die...

I knew that I was badly wounded, because of all the blood, but I didn't know the details. I was in great pain, but the worst of it was the weight of the woman who was leaning heavily on my stomach to staunch the flow of blood. That hurt more than anything else. As I lay there I had no concept of time and was not aware of any noise, though from the amount of activity going on around me it must have been bedlam. People were swarming everywhere. In increasing numbers colleagues kept arriving, peering down at me as they squatted beside me or towered above me. Bill Tillbrook, my lovely inspector at Hornsey, was there, as well as all my colleagues from B-Relief. I began to worry for myself when I noticed the horror on the faces above me. It brought home to me the magnitude of what had happened.

Working as closely as we did together, over the years my colleagues had become my friends. Any police station is a tight-knit community, in which you look after your own, partners against crime. I was one of them. We were like family. And the last thing they wanted was for me to die. It must have been horrific for them to see me lying in that pool of blood. The reality was that West had been preaching on the pavement outside Paradise, giving witness as a lay preacher in the United Apostolic Faith Church. He was telling people that the current fashion of dress, of girls in scanty clothes or wearing underwear on the outside, was leading them into sin. Passers-by reacted in a variety of ways, some making fun of him. When things got out of hand, and he became abusive and threatening, the staff in Paradise had called the police. This kind of public-nuisance incident was our bread and butter, what we were up against daily, and that it had escalated into bloody mayhem is something that most police officers probably fear sporadically in the back of their minds.

I asked Bill where Jeni was and if she was OK. He reassured me that she was, pointing across the pavement to where she sat. He told me not to worry and murmured a few more words of encouragement as he walked off to deal with things. I don't know how long I lay there clinging to Angus's ankles before Sergeant Graham Deal, another old friend, appeared. He had run from one end of the High Road to the other to reach us. As it was unseasonably hot, and he was wearing his suit, he had built up quite a sweat. His salty droplets fell on me as he knelt beside me.

Two ambulances arrived. There was more first aid, in which the helpful passer-by was relieved of her duties. But the pain didn't go away. The paramedics cut off my shirt and applied pads. I'd begun to fade by now as they slid a stretcher beneath me, winched me up and on to a trolley. An air ambulance landed on top of the shopping centre. I heard the whir of the helicopter blades as they wheeled me through the crowds to the blessed calm of the interior of the ambulance. Graham Deal came with me, his sweat still falling on me like reassuring summer rain. Back outside the shopping centre Jeni was ferried after us in a police van, the second road ambulance having broken down with 200,000 miles on the clock. The air ambulance had been a waste of time, because apparently it had been impossible to reach it once it had landed. The last of us to go was John. Eventually a third ambulance transported him down the road to the Whittington at Archway.

One of our ambulance men was particularly nice. I was to meet him again, off and on, and he even came to visit me in hospital after I was shot three years later. He was really amusing that afternoon and kept teasing Graham as he leant over me. 'I think you love her, you're getting so close. You're going to kiss her in a minute,' he said, narrating Graham's every move. It lightened the mood and helped me cope. He kept me cheerful, distracted and awake. I thank him for that.

On arrival at the North Mid we were taken straight

through the swing doors of Casualty to the Crash Area. The police officers who had provided the escort stood around looking concerned. All I could see were yet more worried faces all around me. I was wheeled to one end of the Crash Area, Jeni arrived at the other. I lay on the trolley, and people arrived to peer at me, just as they had when I lay on the pavement. I've never been peered at so much in my life. At one point, Ray Robbins, a PC on B-Relief, popped by. 'You've got a good physique, Helen,' he announced cheerfully, looking me up and down, but by then I was beyond embarrassment or pleasure.

I was in a lot of pain. The doctor and the nurse who were dealing with me were marvellous and explained what they were doing to me every step of the way. The nurse was a lovely woman and kept my spirits up. I felt very locked away and couldn't express anything, and her kindness was releasing for me. Nevertheless I stayed quite calm. I was putting a brave face on it. It was Helen the Police Officer who had been hurt. But when I saw the shoulder wound and caught sight of bone, Helen the Person had to look away.

The nurse started to tend my wounds, dressing them to stem the flow of blood. All the medics were most worried about the stomach wound, so that was investigated first. They opened me up a little, and through a hole in my stomach inserted a tube. Through it they filled my stomach cavity with fluid to establish if I had internal injuries. The next stage, when they rocked the bed back and forth to swish it around inside me, felt a bit Heath Robinson to me. The idea was to find out if there was any blood in the fluid that the nurse then siphoned out, which would indicate possible internal injuries. Fortunately, though it came out pinkish, and I was kept under close observation for the rest of my stay, there was none.

The medical staff were keen to establish exactly the kind of knife that West had used to stab me. They were surprised when they discovered it was a Swiss Army knife and that it had inflicted so much damage. Its effects had been aggravated in that West had not only gone for the soft parts of our bodies but had also used terrific force. There was a mad power behind his punch. If he'd gone for me with a kitchen knife, I don't think I'd be here now.

Some people are not so lucky. WPC Nina Mackay was killed by paranoid schizophrenic Magdi Elgizouli in Stratford, east London, in October 1997 with a single blow from a seven-and-a-half-inch bladed kitchen knife. She was twenty-five, the same age as I was when Rupert West stabbed me. Like West, Elgizouli had a history of irrational and unprovoked violence stretching back over years. Like me, Nina Mackay was a high achiever, in her case dedicated to her job with the TSG. She and her colleagues had been called to a flat in Stratford to arrest Elgizouli for breaching bail conditions. It became necessary for the TSG to break down Elgizouli's door with an enforcer, a heavy metal tube with handles. Mackay was the only officer there trained to use it. She knew the correct procedure and was reminded emphatically that she should step aside once she had forced open the door.

Outside the flat Mackay had some trial runs with the enforcer but found that her upper-body armour restricted her movement. She decided to remove it to take a proper swing at the door. She was nervous because it was the first time she had used the enforcer and was determined not to let down her colleagues. Inside the flat Elgizouli had armed himself with a kitchen knife. Outside, using all her strength, Nina Mackay succeeded in breaking down the door, but was swept along by the momentum of her effort and pushed ahead of the officers with riot shields into the hallway of the flat. She tried to get out of the way, but she couldn't. Elgizouli came at her down the corridor wielding the knife and stabbed her once in the chest right up to the hilt. It makes me go cold just to think about what happened to Nina Mackay, who was obviously a dedicated and fearless woman. It could so easily have been me — or any of the others.

Rupert West had been taken to Wood Green police station, where he was received by Barry as custody officer. To take West to the same station as the one at which the officers he had stabbed were based was insensitive to say the least. It should never have happened. These days, one would hope that he would be taken to one where no one knew personally the officers involved in the incident, but I'm not so sure things have changed.

Barry had been following everything on the radio. Apparently the first he knew of it was Zara's request for urgent assistance, followed by those chilling words, 'We've been stabbed,' which she repeated several times. Barry had responded by alerting every police officer in the area and sending them all in to assist us. Even Mr Morrissey, a chief inspector, booked out a personal radio and came down to the scene. I can hardly imagine what it must have been like for Barry, hearing over the radio all the dreadful things that were happening to people he knew, worked with and cared about, and not knowing the full story, whether they were alive or dead.

Barry had only been a sergeant for a matter of months.

After he'd organised our assistance, he came face to face with the man who had stabbed four of the officers on his relief. Later he had to deal with the woman in the crowd who wanted us all to die. She was brought in screaming. It was very busy at the station that afternoon, and Barry made an immense effort to stay calm as he found himself having to sort everything on his own. West, and anyone else involved, was treated with kid gloves. Barry took great care to write down everything that happened in great detail just in case anyone tried to claim otherwise. He said later that he felt the whole incident had been badly handled because no single person had been in overall control.

Barry had met West before, when he was stationed as a constable on the District Support Unit (DSU) at Holloway, north London, in the mid-eighties. That time West was out sword-waving in public; his weapon was confiscated later from his home under warrant. This sort of behaviour was not what you expected or wanted from anyone, let alone from West, who was built to the same dimensions as a barn door. I had come across him before too, though that September afternoon I was not aware of this. He and his brother had a history of mental illness and were both disturbed. Over the years he had seen several different psychiatrists, none of whom appears to have been able to decide on a diagnosis. Between 1982 and 1989 he received fifteen different diagnoses for his psychiatric condition. Some of the phrases used in reports on him include paranoid schizophrenia, explosive personality disorder, vulnerable personality. There is mention of acute psychotic episodes and confusion states, of alcoholic/drug intoxication. It is clear that he was easily provoked, and the adjective that crops up most frequently is 'aggressive'.

Hornsey Division were certainly aware of his aggression. West was well known to them: he had been arrested on several occasions over the years for criminal damage and possession of offensive weapons. In June 1989 he had assaulted one of its male sergeants after he and another officer had gone to the assistance of a woman whom West had punched when she objected to him barging in front of her in a bus queue. When the police turned up he assaulted two of them, kicking and punching them, and knocking one officer unconscious. This was PS Michael Stanway, who is now medically discharged from the service as a result of a series of injuries that he received in the line of duty. Being booted in the face by Rupert West was just one of a catalogue of hurts that led to his assessment by the Home Office as 75 per cent disabled.

John Davison also had dealings with West during the eighties, at Highbury Corner magistrates' court in north London. He remembers a bear of a man whom he was required to accompany from the cells to the courtroom for a bail hearing. West was sitting in the cell, disturbed and mumbling to himself, getting worked up because he was insistent that he had to get bail. John knew this was unlikely and tried to help him understand this. West's state of mind was clearly irrational, and when bail was refused, it tipped him over the edge and he went berserk; John had help in restraining him on the journey back to the cell. When there was another bail hearing the next week, there was no question of West appearing in court. Instead, the magistrate went to West, who was handcuffed in the back of a police van parked in the yard. West must have caught only a glimpse of the court officials because the van door was opened only long enough for the verdict, bail refused, to be communicated to him. No one hung around for his response this time.

The call at which I had previously encountered West came while I was based in Muswell Hill. We'd been asked to provide back-up to another unit that had been called to an incident at his council flat in Muswell Hill Road. Police were often summoned there: he was always in some sort of trouble. On this occasion he was standing indoors at the top of the flight of stairs that led to the communal hallway, yelling abuse as he hurled furniture at all comers. Eventually, in the summer of 1990, he was evicted on the grounds of causing a nuisance to his neighbours. He considered that he had been harassed. One psychiatric report I have seen suggests that he developed paranoid delusions about his neighbours, saying that they took his mail and swapped around the gas and electricity meters so that he was paying for their gas. At one point he believed they tried to push up the floorboards when he sat down, and that they were helped by the police to put pressure on him. From the time of his eviction until we met him that day in Wood Green he had been living with his younger brother in Tottenham.

The writing was on the wall. Among the small circle in which I moved, no less than three people other than myself had come across him directly. Most people on the division knew about him, or had had dealings with him. He was an accident waiting to happen, a ticking time-bomb. His case highlights the sometimes tragic failure of the Care in the Community scheme that did away with the big psychiatric institutions. Friern Barnet was Hornsey Division's local NHS mental hospital. Once one of the largest asylums in Europe, it followed in the footsteps of a number of redundant mental hospitals whose interesting architecture, spacious accommodation and secluded, landscaped grounds make them ripe for development into upmarket housing. It is now a luxury estate called Princess Park Manor. It had been closed as a hospital under Margaret Thatcher, and West was given a flat in north London and left to look after himself. The psychiatrists only stepped in when things went wrong. This happened regularly. And for Jeni, John and me the consequences of this approach were almost fatal.

The aim of Care in the Community is good in theory but not always in practice. It's fine until the system of care breaks down, which inevitably it does. In 1992 musician Jonathan Zito was stabbed in the head by a schizophrenic on the platform of a London tube station. Later, in Kent, Michael Stone, who was mentally disturbed, had been allowed back into the community because of a legal loophole and murdered Lin and Megan Russell. In a random street attack while he was out walking his dog one Sunday morning Alan Petch, a fifty-year-old father of three, was knifed to death, not far from where we were stabbed, in Holloway, north London, in March 1999. His attacker was a Care in the Community patient. According to the Psychiatric Court Report of March 1992, West was considered to be not agreeable to Care in the Community, but he was allowed back into it on numerous occasions only to return to a mental institution when his health broke down.

In another psychiatric report that followed the stabbing, there was some suggestion that he was suffering from a recurrence of his disturbed state of mind and that his illness had affected his judgement that day. He also had a twin hatred of women and of police officers — one of his brothers said during an interview that he had a bit of a thing about women. Interestingly, he had also wanted to be in the police force and was successful in his application, but because of his mental illness, which manifested itself just before he left school, he did not join up.

Three of the four beat officers who approached West that day were women. Later he said that we had attacked him first with our handcuffs and truncheons, but that he understood that we had done so because we were only doing our job. In his statement he claimed that he had not stabbed us, but that we had fallen on his knife. In his mind what he did was rational. But it was not. And I almost died as a result.

Pat arrived while I was still in the Crash Area. He broke down in tears when he saw me. He had been at home giving Ben his tea when he received a phone call from the control room at the station giving him the bad news. Imagine it! How insensitive! Telling him something like that over the phone! It was disgraceful, and would never have happened to a member of the public, so why it did with a fellow officer I haven't a clue. Surely someone from the Met could have driven over to tell him in person and to transport him the five miles to the hospital. But, no, there he was in shock from the news, with our baby to look after and childcare to organise before he could get to see me. Fortunately we had good neighbours, Yvette and her husband, Mike, who came over to the flat to take care of Ben while Pat made his own way to the North Mid.

I had other visitors, too, that evening. The Met's then commissioner, Peter Imbert, took the time to put in an appearance. The fact that the national press were encamped on the pavement outside the hospital might have had something to do with his presence. There was massive media interest, with TV cameras and all the press and their paraphernalia making it difficult for everyday life at the hospital to function normally. I found him a genuine and sympathetic person, and my eyes filled with tears as he sat by my bedside and held my hand. He also visited the Whittington, where John was so overcome by his presence and support that he couldn't stop himself sobbing. The commissioner took it in his stride. Months later, when the two men met in a lift at New Scotland Yard, he remembered John and what had happened to us all that day.

Yvette took Ben to our child-minder, Hilary, for the night then came down to the hospital to see me and reassure Pat that everything was under control at home. It turned out she knew my nurse, and they gossiped and exchanged phone numbers over my head. Life goes on, I thought. I don't know how long I remained in the Crash Area while they patched me up and prepared me for surgery. At some stage, though, Pat phoned my parents. Later I was to discover that something rather extraordinary had happened with them.

The previous afternoon my father had been mowing the lawn in the orchard of the garden at Half Acre. When he reached the spot beside the apple trees where the wedding photographer had taken the official photos of Pat and me, he had a premonition, a flash of warning about me that involved a knife. It felt dangerous and uncomfortable. My father is a man of few words, and that afternoon he felt foolish that his mind was playing tricks on him and told himself not to be so daft. The next day Pat phoned with the news. Dad spent the next few hours out in the garden, pacing up and down his rows of beans, tut-tutting and sighing, his brain working overtime. His sole thought was that he wanted to kill West and anyone else who had, might or would ever hurt me. He felt murderous.

My mother, as usual, kept her feelings to herself. She is not the weeping and wailing type, so much so that it sometimes seems almost as if she doesn't care. But of course she does, and when she heard the news that afternoon her insides went all tight and she started a migraine. She tells me now that she felt devastated. That waiting for further news long into the night was intolerable. Their car was under repair in the local garage, so they had to hang on until the mechanics rallied round the following morning and got it fixed. With some sweet peas from our local vicar Tony Lee, who'd picked them for me specially from his garden, and good wishes from all my family and friends, my mother drove up to London to be with me.

I was taken up to the ward to await my turn in the operating theatre, into which I was wheeled around ten that night. My wounds were so deep they required several layers of stitches. Fortunately that was all that was required. I came round from the anaesthetic in the early hours of Tuesday morning to find myself back on the ward with Pat at my bedside. There he stayed to comfort me until sleep took over, and he left to get what rest he could. When I woke up the next day my first thought was, Thank God I had those two bowls of Ready Brek before I went to work yesterday.

I was in agony. I never found out whether or not I had broken any ribs, but it was terribly painful just to sit up in bed. The arm wounds penetrated to the bone. It hadn't looked much on the outside, but that wasn't where it counted. I was later told that I was lucky not to have died. The place where I'd been stabbed in the abdomen was a millimetre from my spleen and very close to a major blood vessel. This struck me hard: not only might I have died but my ten-month-old baby would have been motherless.

On the Wednesday, B-Relief, including Barry, came in to see Jeni and me in the ward, where we'd been installed in an annex. They brought cards and queued up by our beds to give us encouragement and a hug. John was still in the Whittington, where Pat went to visit him, taking him a pair of socks as a get-well present.

From then until we left we received constant attention, along with flowers and cards, chocolates and books. I was sent a sweet little notelet of a kitten proffering a rosy-red apple from someone who signed himself A. Prisoner. It came from E Wing of HMP Littlehey in Cambridgeshire, and this is what it said: 'A very great number of the inmates here were appalled to read of your injuries, and I just wanted to tell you that even the so-called *real* villains are disgusted by what has happened to you and your colleagues ... I realise that we in jail are not considered part of the general public, but nevertheless you have our support and our very best wishes for a speedy recovery.'

We were inundated with presents from people we knew and people we didn't. Commenting on the hostility from certain elements of the crowd towards us that day, John Davison later remarked that it was more than counterbalanced by all those who sent flowers, cards and good wishes to us in hospital. In fact, we had so many flowers that we had to give them away. Also we were never left alone to rest and recover. Looking back, it was almost as if we had become a possession of the Met because of what had happened to us. I remember Pat complaining that he and I were never alone for even five minutes. There were constant visits from senior officers and other officials.

The press were outside, radio, TV and all the national newspapers, but wanted to be allowed on to the ward to interview us. It was a hive of activity. The media had to be dealt with, and a press conference was arranged. TV cameras and all the other broadcasting paraphernalia were wheeled in. I felt awful. I felt sick. I didn't really want to talk to anyone. It was the day after I'd been stabbed, and I needed to rest. However, although it wasn't something I thought consciously, when you're a police officer, you do what you think is the right thing, and you go through with what's asked of you.

Consequently that evening and the next day we found ourselves on the television news and in all the national newspapers. There were headlines in the *Daily Mirror*, 'Maniac Stabs Three WPCs', the *Sun*, 'Bloody But Unbeaten', the *Daily Mail*, 'Knifeman Stabs 3 Girl PCs' and so on, plus follow-up pieces in which Jeni and I presented a united front. In the *Daily Star* they talked of 'The Two Faces Of Courage', and there was that photo of us side by side in our hospital beds with Jeni leaning over to comfort me. We both agreed that it was the fantastic support of the public and our colleagues that made our job such a joy. We had only one thing on our minds, apparently: 'We just want to get back to work,' we said in unison. The *Mail*, under a header 'Husbands Agree With Heroines Who Accept Danger' continued the perpetual theme of 'Stabbed WPCs Want To Be Back On Their Beat'. Yes, that's what we said. And we meant it.

But was it a suitable job for a woman? they wanted to know. Yes, it was, we replied. Were we as women especially at risk? they asked. No, we were not, we answered. Jeni replied for both of us when she said: 'We wear the same uniform, and we do the same job as the men.' Our husbands backed us up. Jeni's Mark, a sergeant with the Met, was asked whether or not his wife should reconsider her career and replied, 'Certainly not.' Pat was reported as saying: 'We haven't spoken openly about the risks, but we both know you can get injured. But if you thought about it too hard you'd never go to work in the morning. Helen is very career-minded, probably the better half of our team, and we have got high expectations for her prospects.'

At the time I saw none of the press coverage, nor did I want to. I hadn't felt at ease about the media cosying up to our bedsides, and I felt even less so after what happened when they had gone. The press had been admitted to our ward in batches. When the first lot left, and we were preparing ourselves for the TV cameras, one of our chief inspectors, Mr Morrissey, found a tape-recorder near our beds that was still recording. He removed the tape and disposed of it, not sure whether it was a deliberate ploy to catch us out or just an oversight. Who knows?

Thankfully, our relief were wonderfully supportive. Not for nothing were B-Relief called the Gummy Bears. This was the name the other reliefs had given us over the years because we were famous for being friendly and hugging each other and everybody else at the least excuse. One day we were taken from the ward in wheelchairs, supposedly on a visit to the dressings clinic, only to find ourselves in a room with three of the Chippendales, where they just chatted to us. Fortunately there was no floorshow. I couldn't have stood that. The cast of *The Bill* sent us autographed photos. Earl Ferrers, the Home Office minister for the police, came to see us. He also visited the station, where some of the officers told him a few home truths. He was particularly shocked at the reaction of the public at the scene of the stabbing. He'd thought that passers-by would run to our aid, and I think he found it hard to credit the reality.

Some people it was wonderful to see. Such as Barry. Others I could have done without. I felt I was in a media circus. It was all too much. It is good publicity for the police to show their injured officers lying in a hospital bed. They get the sympathy vote. It was not good for me. I was in shock and traumatised. I didn't realise this at the time, though I didn't like the hoops through which I had to jump. I just did it. Since I have seen this happening to others, I realise it's not the right thing when you've been a victim of crime, when you've gone through an experience that is beyond the everyday. But that's what they do. Through the press exposure of such incidents, the police service is saying, 'Our officers were doing their job well and look what's happened to them.' Obviously the public should be made aware of what goes on in the course of police work, but not by parading the victims. Because at the end of the day, although you are a police officer, you are also a victim. I didn't fully realise the implications of this, thinking, I'll be back at work in a fortnight.

Pat came to pick me up when I was discharged from the North Mid that weekend. When he got me home my mum was there where she had been all week, going back and forth to visit me and between times staying at our flat to look after Ben. I hadn't seen Ben since before the stabbing. I didn't feel there was much point in subjecting him to the rigours of a strange place and his mummy lying in a hospital bed. In the flat there were flowers everywhere, from neighbours, friends and colleagues. I had even more cards to open. It was great for a day or two, but then I started to realise that, while I'd been the centre of attention for a week, I had now to face the real aftermath of the stabbing. I felt very alone. I really wanted to speak to Barry. He was such an easy person for me to talk to. And I did, from time to time, but it was difficult to arrange from home.

I was under the weather, but not bed bound. I walked over to see friends who had left me flowers, and that was about it. Above all, though, I was a mum, and I had Ben to look after. My home life couldn't grind to a halt because of my injuries. My mother stayed on for a few days and helped us out. Pat had been given compassionate leave so he was there for me too. But I wasn't finding it easy, in all sorts of ways. I was still very much the police officer, that was so much of my life, and I guess that because of it I felt I still had to remain reasonably calm. People had that image of me, and I had it of myself. I was very capable at work, but when you get home, the façade cracks. Then you have to deal not only with the injured person inside the uniform but also with how your family has been affected.

Pat and I hadn't been particularly happy before, and the stabbing and its aftermath drove a deeper wedge between us instead of bringing us closer. The mental stress was enormous. Not surprisingly, Pat bore the brunt of it. But he wasn't able to cope. He had been badly injured himself at Broadwater Farm, and he'd always worried about me being out on the front line. Now his worst fears had become a reality. Of course, you just don't understand what's happening to you: you are too close to it. I had never heard of post-traumatic stress disorder (PTSD). Stress was something that affected other people; it wasn't something I had to think about.

Our stabbing became a force for radical change in police policy. John Davison was largely behind this. He had been a police officer for more than ten years and was on the third carrier of the DSU (District Support Unit) into Broadwater Farm during the riots. He knew about PTSD from that time and had grasped then how difficult it was to tackle. Dealing with traumatised people is extremely tricky, and it is hard to give the right response because everyone's needs and experiences are different. Around the time of the stabbing he was spending some time on secondment to Bramshill, the police training college in Hampshire, on accelerated promotion, expected to make fast progress up the rungs of the Met's career ladder. He was going places fast. But he was becoming aware of the price he would pay for this.

Immediately after he'd disarmed West, John slumped to the pavement like a rag doll and started to sob, all his energy suddenly gone. He had no option but to give in. He was seriously injured, and no one could, or would, blame him for doing so. But as the senior officer at the scene he felt torn. All his training told him to carry on, to give first aid, comfort and encouragement. He was responsible. But sometimes all the training and best intentions in the world can't help when you're facing impossible odds.

Sergeant Davison the officer had done enough, and he was starting to face what had happened to him that afternoon. He was not ready for the vulnerability he experienced when the ambulance crew arrived and began to cut through his uniform. This made him feel intolerably exposed, and with the image of his authority stripped away with the veneer of his uniform John Davison the man went immediately into shock. When he first told me about this I recalled how vulnerable I, too, had felt as I lay in the street while the paramedics cut through my shirt to tend to my wounds. It had been the strangest feeling.

When he was stabbed that day in Wood Green, John was married and his daughter Charlotte was only five weeks old. He was to spend the next four months with his wife and new baby. During that time he went through the gamut of emotions from guilt that he could have done more to exhilaration at having survived, and just how great it was to be alive. Nevertheless he felt frail and apprehensive about going out, largely because his stomach wound was still painful and increased his sense of vulnerability. Little things got to him, such as the day when a bunch of loudmouth lads came strutting towards him along the street and he felt petrified.

In an attempt to build up his strength again, as soon as he was able John returned to the gym to train. Using only light weights at first, he was determined to get back to the peak of health and fitness. Like me, he believes that one of the reasons we both survived our physical injuries so well and recovered so fast is because we were both so fit and our bodies able to heal quickly. But mentally it was a different story, and for months after he was stabbed John suffered from a recurring image that came to him without warning of a knife that went continually in and out of a belted torso clad in a white Met shirt. Although it might seem obvious to an outsider, John couldn't make head or tail of it for a long time. One day it finally dawned on him that he was seeing himself being stabbed. He was reliving and processing West's assault.

John went back to work in January 1992. With his GP he had worked out a plan to break himself in gently, but light duties were not part of it. He felt he needed to jump in at the deep end and nip in the bud any doubts he might have about the job. For him it was sink or swim. And he swam. On his first day back B-Relief presented him with his hat. It had been retrieved from the gutter by one of them on the day of the stabbing, since when it had been locked in the safe for John's return. John was as touched by this as he was amused to discover his sandwiches still in the fridge from when he had placed them there at the beginning of his shift on 2 September, four months earlier.

Going back to work was a huge psychological leap for John and brought back lots of memories for him, as it did for me. He was giving a talk one day to his course at Bramshill when he reached the part where he was describing his behaviour after he'd been stabbed and disarmed West. He was beginning to say how upset he'd been at his inability to carry on and take control of the incident — something he expected of himself as sector sergeant — when suddenly he broke down in tears. This elicited great sympathy from his audience, and they all took a break to give him time to recover. He, like me, felt vulnerable for a long time. There was even a rumour circulating, though I heard no word of it, that some officers on the division were so scared on the streets that they began to consider taking their own defensive measures.

Dealing with the public made John especially uneasy. His first arrest made him panic so much that he was too terrified to mention to his prisoner that he was under arrest until they were back in the relative safety of the station. I understood this. Amongst all this readjustment, John spent a lot of time thinking about what had happened to us all that September afternoon. He felt sure that there could have been a less damaging outcome for us all if West had been handled differently at the time, and that getting involved, as we were all expected to do, should not mean ignoring your own safety and being hurt.

When John first mooted his ideas for an officer-safety guide to the Met, he was greeted by a deafening silence. But he carried on regardless, gathering material on an assortment of police forces from all over the world, a total of thirty law-enforcement agencies in eight countries. He felt that the Met had a lot to learn from America, that what police officers were experiencing on the streets of London in the 1980s was similar to what had been going on in New York in the 1970s. Then a huge number of officers had lost their lives on patrol.

Pilot schemes in operation in America were calling it officer survival, and the key to it all was for an officer to look professional, smart and in control when approaching a member of the public. They should also have a generally heightened awareness and a good attitude, the recognition that there was no such thing as a routine or low-risk situation. Only two categories applied in police work: high risk or unknown risk. On one occasion in south London a man was stopped for kerb crawling and arrested for drunk-driving after being breathalysed. During the booking-in process back at the station a controlled drug fell out of his pocket. As an officer bent down to retrieve it, the prisoner pulled a loaded handgun from the waistband of his trousers and pointed it at the custody sergeant. It was only thanks to the prompt action of the other officers present — one of whom courageously pushed his thumb in front of the firing hammer — that the man was overpowered. The gun was found to contain enough bullets to have killed every PC in the room. The prisoner, it transpired, was wanted for a series of armed robberies across the south of England.

It was this kind of alarming anecdote that inspired John to continue, and he built up a dossier of facts and figures, some of which were surprising. A police officer was more likely to be seriously injured or killed on patrol than as a member of a special team, such as the ARVs, the armed response vehicles to which I later belonged. Some third of all assaults took place before police officers even had a chance to talk to a suspect, as ours had. Officers on uniformed patrol sustained 78 per cent of assaults, with 60 per cent occurring on the streets. Of all the injuries sustained by the police 25 per cent were at the point of arrest or after a suspect had been detained. Just like ours. If we wanted to stay alive on the streets we had to approach things differently. The message was that we were never safe, and we had always to remember that.

When John told the Met that he planned to publish his findings privately, they began to take notice of him. By then he was working with Mike Tween and Bill Fox, and in November 1994 they asked me to help. The result was a teaching programme piloted with 5 Area in south-west London, its officers some of the old sweats, the hard nuts, who believed that nothing could change their lot. When even they applauded it, the Met had no option but to pay up and shut up. *The Good Practice Guide to Officer Safety* is the title of the Met book and the video that came out of it. It outlined a radical new approach to officer survival on the streets. It cost the Met £28 million to re-educate its officers according to its guidelines. The up-side is that today its officers are taught to give priority to their personal safety.

I think this was a valuable lesson to learn, though I don't believe it would have changed our experience with Rupert West that day in 1991. As the first officer to approach him, I'm not sure there was much I could have done differently. Nothing led me to believe that he was going to react so violently. With the benefit of hindsight the only thing I might have given more consideration to was the fact that he had his back to me. This should have made me more aware. I couldn't see what he was doing or what he had in his hands. If you can't see a suspect's hands you may well be gambling with your life. But it's a difficult issue because society very much dictates how officers deal with the public, and even if he had been facing me I wouldn't have stood much of a chance without my baton drawn. In the US it's OK for officers to employ weapons a lot more, to draw their guns. It's all much more defensive from the start. I don't imagine the British public would appreciate being approached by a police officer with baton drawn. But things are changing. And they were about to for me then. Big-time.

I had physiotherapy and ultrasound treatment on my scars, which took me back to the environs of Hendon Police Training School. The Met ran a nursing home there that dealt with its sick and injured officers, and offered a range of medical services. I also returned to the North Mid ten days after the stabbing to have the stitches taken out. The depth of the laceration in my upper forearm had affected my little finger on the injured left arm; the knife had apparently cut through muscle fibres. It didn't work properly, and I couldn't really move it; it just hung on my hand as if it didn't belong there. That was a worry, but they offered me physiotherapy and told me it would come right in time. It has, virtually, but even now my grip is weaker with that hand. One of the stab wounds on my left upper arm healed in ugly ridges, and I became self-conscious and embarrassed about it. I was a young woman who enjoyed having an attractive body, and I would no longer be able to wear a sleeveless dress or blouse without the scar showing. It was just a small thing, but added to the rest it had an adverse effect on my general well-being.

Although I wouldn't say I was depressed, there were more and more problems between Pat and me, and I was becoming increasingly involved with and reliant on Barry. The day the stitches came out, Pat and I had arranged to see everyone at Wood Green station. B-Relief were going to be on that day, and I was dying to see them, especially Barry. I wanted to say hello and show them I was all right — not that they needed telling. None of them had any doubt that I would be fine. I even recall Ray Robbins saying that he wasn't sure about the others but that I would be all right. 'Helen's really tough,' he said confidently. That was the image people had of me and I had of myself. Even the medical report by consultant psychiatrist R. S. Mackinnon, which followed in 1993 as part of my criminal-injuries claim after the stabbing, confirmed this: 'I suspect that Mrs Barnett is one who would underplay her symptoms and difficulties.'

At that stage as far as I was concerned I'd just suffered physical injuries. I wasn't aware of the mental trauma, though Mackinnon thought differently and said so in no uncertain terms: 'The original cause of her mental injury and disablement was clearly the incident on 2 September 1991, and she has clearly not recovered from that.' He added: 'Given her basic personality, it seems a pity that she was not given the appropriate psychological debriefing and support later. With that, I believe that she would have made a better recovery from such a traumatic event and might even have avoided most of the post-traumatic stress disorder that she has suffered.'

That's what he thought. And he was right. But at that point in the autumn of 1991 to me it was going to be simple. I'd be back at work in a matter of weeks. For the moment at least Helen the Wounded Person was refusing to emerge from behind the Super WPC.

CHAPTER 6

DISTRESS, BULIMIA AND DIVORCE

I didn't wake up one morning and think, Eureka! I know what's wrong. It was subtler than that and it emerged slowly in a variety of ways: bulimia, the arguing at home and a fanatical obsession with training and physical fitness that verged on the addictive. Despite my best intentions I did not return to work for nine months. I thought I'd simply sustained straightforward, albeit serious, physical injuries. But the damage went deeper: I had no idea how deep.

No one would ever describe me as a girly type, and as a child I was a bit of a tomboy. I felt emotionally resilient. I could deal with the everyday horrors of police life, as I could with my recent ordeal. I was the hardy sort. I subscribed to this image of myself. In part I revelled in it: in part I did not. Out in public I wore my mask. Behind it I was finding things difficult and needed more and more energy just to keep going. I wasn't aware at this stage that I'd been psychologically affected, traumatised, by the stabbing. At home, though we had never found it especially easy to communicate, relations between Pat and me got worse. I spent a lot of time in the gym, returning there as soon as the stitches were removed to cycle and work out. I had ten days off from fitness training, that was all. I continued to push myself until it hurt, and further. On one occasion a while later I went to the police gym in Hendon to have my fitness assessed. They use a chart, divided by gender, age, height and so on, to show your ideal level of fitness. I was so fit that I was off the chart.

I didn't sit down and pronounce one day that psychologically as well as physically my encounter with Rupert West had left its scars. It just doesn't work like that. It is only since I have left the Met that the jigsaw has begun to fit together. Then I was in pieces. It could have been avoided if we had been treated differently.

From the day we left hospital to the day we returned to work, our aftercare was insufficient. The Job, as we called the Met, should have done something more for us. If you rang the Met today to ask them about their aftercare for injured officers, they'd tell you they have a system in place to deal with it. And this is true. But what is also true, in my view, is that it isn't as good as it should be, and there's still not enough specialist aftercare. We needed help to recover properly from what had happened to us. We needed to understand that there is sometimes a stress reaction to emotional shock following physical trauma, the anxiety disorder known as PTSD. Someone should have given us an idea of what to look out for, of the ways in which we might be affected. I now know the list of possible symptoms like the back of my hand: nightmares, obsessive thoughts that won't go away, hypervigilance, irritability, anger. I suffered from all of these. For years I had a recurring dream about being stabbed in the throat, of my throat filling up with blood. If it didn't shock me awake in the night, the following morning I would get up feeling worn out. I might have slept all night, but I was too exhausted to function properly. Someone might have warned us that we weren't going mad if we had sleep difficulties, felt tired most of the time or on the edge of tears, depressed, started to drink more or rely on drugs. I recognised all this too, though being so obsessive about my physical health I never resorted to drink or drugs.

PTSD can affect a person's self-esteem, their relationships with others at work and at home. Increased anxiety can lead to a breakdown in relationships, especially at home. Colleagues may find it difficult to work alongside you because of this or because of your anger at the smallest things. All of this should have been made clear to us. All of this happened to me. At home my marriage, admittedly shaky before I was stabbed, collapsed under the strain. At night I suffered from restless sleep and nightmares. I was lucky because once I'd started work again I was so exhausted from shift work, training in the gym and looking after Ben that I usually managed to sleep fairly well. But it was never a nourishing sleep, I never felt rested, and I would wake up feeling as tired as if I hadn't been to bed. In my sleep I started to grind my teeth.

These were among the physical reactions I experienced to stress, though there were others. I found it hard to concentrate. I could never sit down and relax. I was always cleaning the house or doing something. Perhaps even the studying for the sergeants' exams, which I embarked on soon after my return to work, was a way of concentrating my mind on something else, of distracting me from my distress. Excessive gym training was part of it too. I've since learnt that this is one way of coping with all the adrenaline that the body produces under stress. At work, I found I would check and recheck the tiniest details on the way to a call, which drove me mad, and probably my colleagues too. I'd feel anxious for no reason. Out on patrol my heart would be racing, though I was calm on the outside. But most especially we did not have instilled in us the understanding that the way I and the others felt was quite normal, and that these were perfectly understandable human responses to an intolerable circumstance.

But at that time I didn't think I needed help. I didn't think I had a problem. To get help you have to identify that there is something with which you need help. Stress wasn't something to which I'd ever admit, never mind something about which I'd seek counselling or therapy. It was a dirty word that came under 'weak' in my vocabulary. In the job it was not, and probably still is not, acceptable to admit to feeling stressed. I think about the serial involved in the Broadwater Farm riots. Undoubtedly they were affected by what they saw, including Pat, who went back to work within two days. There was nothing in place to support any of them. The form was that once the Met had established that you weren't going to die on them, they would parade your injuries to the world to gain public sympathy. Then they'd give you a few days off to recover, offer you a little helping hand in the form of Welfare, and then the chief medical officer (CMO) gives you a date by which to return to work. The CMO does that and only that, based on doctors' reports and what you tell them.

After I returned home from hospital, Welfare contacted me, in the shape of retired PC Mick Simms. He was nice enough, but I believe he was not adequately trained by the Met in all the details and complexities his role entailed. He told me kindly that if there was anything I needed to discuss, then I should please give him a ring. I also received a personal letter from Mr Harvey, the chief superintendent of Hornsey Division, offering his sympathy and giving me his home telephone number if I needed anything, even just to talk. This was very kind of him, but it wasn't likely that I'd ever have taken him up on his offer. I didn't know him from Adam and, feeling as I did, phoning him was the last thing I'd have wanted or felt able to do. I was also encouraged to go to Bushey Sports Club for debriefing — what they now term Defuse — a couple of weeks after I'd come out of hospital. This was supposed to help me establish what exactly happened on Mad Monday, and why we did what we did, quelling any rumour or assumptions about our behaviour that day. It should have been a safe place for us to vent our feelings and talk things through, to let off steam, which might have helped to put paid to any long-term problems. But the Bushey debrief turned itself into a photo opportunity for the *Job*, the Met's in-house magazine. I was gobsmacked, but by that time I had no resources with which to resist and felt obliged to comply.

The Met eventually offered me a course in aikido at Hendon. This was what they considered appropriate treatment for an officer wounded in the course of duty. Is that what's really best for an injured, possibly traumatised officer? The message is, 'Well, it's happened to you once, so why not be prepared next time?' I didn't find it a suitable way to alleviate anxiety and restore your faith in life and in yourself. After a few weeks I refused to attend because I found it such a waste of time. It didn't help me sort myself out at all.

What happened later didn't help much either. It was early 1996 that I found out about the video that accompanied the *Good Practice Guide to Officer Safety*, part of which re-enacted our stabbings. No one had contacted or consulted me about it: in it we three WPCs are portrayed as a bunch of bimbos who don't know our right hand from our left. What was worse was that I got wind of the fact that in an officer-safety class discussion of the video, critical comments were made about how, according to the reconstruction, we behaved that day. The video was eventually withdrawn from use but not without a fight. I felt very let down, and this was hardly surprising. We were never treated as victims, there was little aftercare and the needs of the Met were put above our own.

No form of rehabilitation followed for any of us. It seems to be a not uncommon approach to officers injured in the line of duty. PS Michael Stanway gets angry when he hears the media reporting what he calls Sir Paul Condon's ill-founded belief that officers who retire because of injuries received while serving the public are ripping off the system. He believes that the present problems plaguing the Met, especially with regard to personnel and health matters, have been caused by incompetent, badly trained management, especially since police officers have been removed from administrative posts and replaced by civil servants. He feels strongly about the apparent preference of the government and the Home Office to spend all their time and public money on the welfare of criminals and terrorists rather than on the victims of crime. He has a point.

But before our long, unhappy saga had fully unfolded, in March 1992, nearly seven months after the stabbing, we had to contend with the trial of our assailant, Rupert West, at the Old Bailey. As the date drew closer, it was increasingly difficult to cope. I just soldiered on, pretty much alone, although eventually I was to have a run-in with possibly well-meaning but none the less incompetent counsellors. At one point, much later, I was promised an opportunity to talk to the Met's occupational-health advisers to tell them how inadequate the system and guidelines had proved for me. I didn't relish the prospect, but I wanted to try my best to ensure that other officers were treated with the care and compassion that I felt had been lacking in my case. I was promised time and time again that I would have the opportunity to speak to a team of occupational-health advisers, but nothing ever materialised.

When the day of the trial dawned, the four of us found ourselves together again for the first time since the stabbing and the Bushey debrief, and very much on our own. There were no senior officers present, apart from Detective Inspector Michael Rutter, the SO dealing with the case, and not a single welfare officer to give us one scrap of support. The press, however, were out in full. It got worse. Once inside the courtroom we, the victims, were ushered to a sunken seating area, a sort of dugout, directly in front of the judge, who was looking down on us. Worst of all was the moment they produced Rupert West from the court cells and put him in the dock immediately behind us. With a guard at his side he towered above us. I could feel his presence, and it chilled me. That certainly didn't help my already fragile state of mind.

On 3 September, the day after the stabbing, West had appeared before Haringey magistrates on four charges of attempted murder. Now, we sat and listened as the attempted murder charge was modified via some legal plea bargaining to grievous bodily harm. That was upsetting in itself, hearing us all discussed like that, bartering, it seemed, over our distress. Rationally we understood that attempted murder is a difficult charge to prove because of the requirement to prove intent. Given West's mental state, proving intent would have been well-nigh impossible, so there was a better chance of conviction with GBH with intent. But I felt emotionally betrayed by this. I also felt cheated that, because West had pleaded guilty, I was not required to give evidence. I guess I had wanted my say. When West stood above us to read out his apology, John

Davison told me later that from the expression on my face he thought I was going to leap out of our pit and punch the man. Obviously I looked as angry as I felt. West's apology was scripted. It was legal window-dressing. He was too far gone on prescription drugs to know what was happening in that courtroom that day. Funnily enough, apart from appearing as if I wanted to punch out his lights at that moment, I did not and do not have any strong feelings about Rupert West. I don't hate him and I don't feel angry with him for what he did to me. My father wanted to kill him, as he paced the rows of beans when he heard that I'd been stabbed, so he has acted out for me any feelings of revenge I might have had. It's odd, really, but I do know that if anyone ever hurt either of my children, they would have a snowball in hell's chance of survival.

At the Central Criminal Court we watched him, his voice heavy with medication, put through his paces. At one point he lost it, and started to shout his apologies at us for, as he put it, 'losing my temper in public'. He had to be prompted to answer 'Not Guilty' to each charge of attempted murder and 'Guilty' to the charge of GBH. At the end of the day he was convicted and sent to a secure unit at Rampton special hospital in Northamptonshire. It was an incredibly emotional time, which we had to live through largely on our own with little support. If we'd had a senior officer in court with us it is likely that we would have been better treated. However you fare on such occasions, everyone needs someone to fight their corner. There was some acknowledgement from the prosecutor, John Bevan, who said at one point: 'The psychological trauma of such an episode must be considerable, and the fact they have borne it so well is a great credit to them.'

Conversely, we found the CPS unsympathetic on the whole and their attitude dismissive. It was the justice system at its worst, just going through the motions. After the trial we four ran from the courtroom to an antechamber nearby with the press in hot pursuit. We were all, except John, in tears. It had been a harrowing day, especially seeing and hearing Rupert West. Later, when we'd calmed down, we posed for a press photo outside the Old Bailey. Then we went back to Hornsey in a minibus driven by John before we went our separate ways. From that day to this I have tried to forget. I have never read any of the case papers or trial transcripts or anything like that. I know that John and Jeni have found this helpful, but I wanted to shut the door on it all and avoid any reruns as far as I could. There's no problem too big to run away from.

Rupert West's trial was reported in several newspapers, including my local *Cheshunt and Waltham Mercury*. On the front page, next to the piece about me, 'Brave WPC Helen' — always that adjective to describe me — there was another story: 'Lucy Joins The Met'. Lucy, aged eleven, had joined The Met on Trading Places Day. She was interested in a career in the police service and had taken the opportunity to stand in for WPC Cathy Bingle one Friday morning. In the afternoon it was Cathy's turn to go back to school and sit behind a desk for lessons in the classroom of Brooklands Junior School. A spokesman at the station said afterwards that the exchange had been a great success. I wondered then, and I wonder now, what I'd have said to Lucy. I'd started with high hopes too.

With the trial behind us, life had to go on. But it was not life as I had known it. I was highly commended in the Central Criminal Court for my behaviour on the day of the

On patrol during Prince Andrew's wedding, pictured here with PC Ryan David, at the time the most highly decorated officer in the Met.

Top: 1984, as a cadet at Hendon Police Training School.

Bottom: The Passing Out parade at Hendon in January 1986. I am being awarded with the shield for top student. I also received the Baton of Honour.

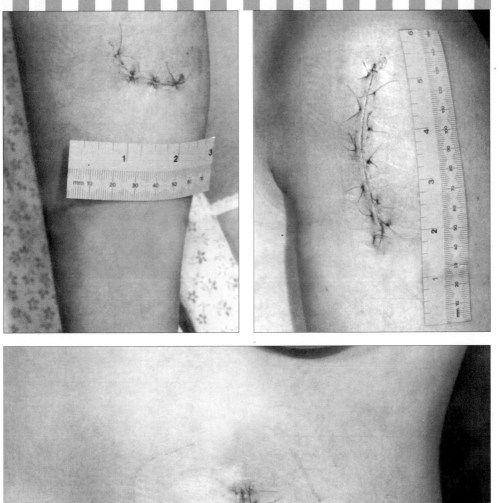

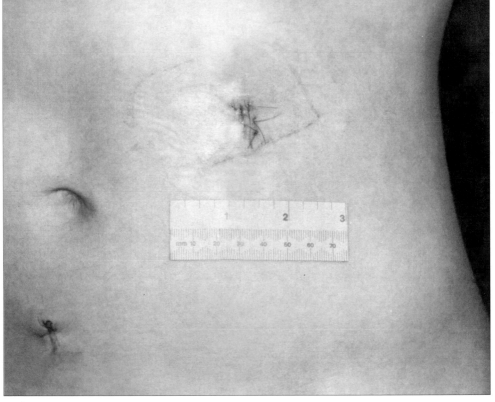

The injuries received when psychiatric patient Rupert West stabbed me twice in the arm and once in the abdomen, dangerously close to a major blood vessel.

Chief Superintendent's Commendation

Awarded to

P.C Helen Barnett

for

*Courage and determination when
dealing with an armed suspect.*

30 9/93.
_____
Date

Terence Shlr
_____
Chief Superintendent

M.P.90

Just two of the
Commendations I
received in the
course of duty.

By the QUEEN'S Order the name of

*Police Constable
Helen Frances Barnett
Metropolitan Police*
was published in the London Gazette on
1st July 1994
as commended for brave conduct.
I am charged to express Her Majesty's
high appreciation of the service rendered.

John Major.

Prime Minister and First Lord
of the Treasury

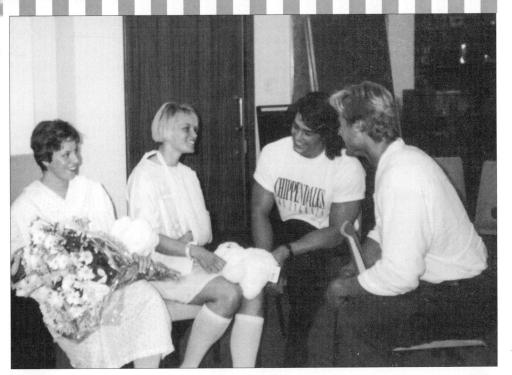

Top: While recovering in hospital after the stabbing, Jeni Lawson and I were visited by the Chippendales.

Bottom: Receiving a Queen's Commendation, flanked by Lord Bramall (left) and Sir Paul Condon.

Posing for a press photo outside the Old Bailey after Rupert West's trial there in March 1990. With me are two other officers who were also stabbed at the time.

Firearms practice with a Heckler & Koch (*top*) and Glock pistol (*below*), at the specially equipped underground firing range at Holborn Police station.

With my husband Steve, son Ben and daughter Molly in July 1997. I had just received
an Assistant Commissioner Commendation for my conduct during the shooting
in 1994. My life has moved on, with my family as its focus now, though despite the
smiles the memories linger.

stabbing and for the part I played at the scene of the crime. It was good to hear, but it didn't help much. I was way off tack, and the only person I could talk to frankly and with whom I could allow myself the luxury of being me was Barry. I was off sick from September 1991 until the following May. During that time my marriage fell apart. It was Pat who wanted us to stay together: I was the one who initiated the split, which was sealed with a kiss.

During September and throughout the autumn I had begun to see more and more of Barry. I'd been round to his flat in Enfield for a cup of coffee and a chat shortly after the stabbing and before my stitches came out. At work we had talked all the time, and I missed that. I also had plenty to talk about. It was really nice to catch up, because, if nothing else, he was my friend. But there *was* something else: I was enormously attracted to Barry, and we'd hit it off from the start. He was such a lovely, unusual man. Part of me still didn't want to hurt Pat — he was my husband after all, even though we weren't particularly happy, and Ben's father. It was such a difficult decision to make, compounded by what had happened at work.

Barry admired me, the sort of person I was, how I dealt with other people. He made me feel good about myself and helped me believe in myself. Even now when I have to make a decision about something I occasionally think, What would Barry say? There were problems in our relationship, which became apparent over time, but at that point it was good for me and incredibly supportive. He would always find an opportunity to compliment me. I found all of this very attractive.

By October our affair had begun with that kiss, one day when I was visiting Barry at home. I was swept off my feet by him, although it must be said that I wasn't standing on firm ground to start with. Though I was outwardly calm, inwardly I was seething, and I found that he was always there for me, always wise, sensitive and understanding, ready to listen. He helped me through what was, frankly, a crazy time.

I'd been dieting for a while and was always conscious of what I ate because of my commitment to gym work and training. As a body-builder, Pat was keen on nutrition and aware of what food he should and shouldn't eat. When I'd first met him he was involved in selling the dietary regime HerbaLife, and right from the start watching what we ate was part and parcel of our life together. There is a fine line between this and an eating disorder. I crossed that line and became bulimic when Pat left towards the end of the year. The bulimia developed after I'd been stabbed. Although eating gave me comfort, afterwards I felt discomforted by it. I am still prone to going for the biscuits if I'm a bit fed up. But at that point I was more than a bit fed up. My life was spinning out of orbit.

I was on the edge of becoming obsessed with training and having a fit body, and comfort-eating biscuits did not tally with that. After a binge I used to make myself throw up. Like any kind of eating disorder, bulimia brings up control issues, and the one thing I felt I could control was what I ate. I could not cope with all the change I was undergoing, and bulimia was my way of dealing with it. It only developed when I found myself at home facing all the problems I had kept at bay before by losing myself in my job — all the dissatisfactions that couldn't be defused by work, my big high, where I was a capable person who always got stuck in and got results. I could no longer hide behind the external identity that work brings, even though I knew I was going to go back some time.

Later, when I saw the interview she gave on TV, I thought it took a lot of courage for Princess Diana to talk about her experiences of bulimia. I admired her for that. It opened the gates for a lot of other people to admit to their problems and do something about them, including me. Barry knew I was bulimic, and apart from him the only other person I mentioned it to was the physiotherapist I was seeing at the injuries clinic at Hendon. He didn't seem very informed about it and, though he tried to help with some relaxation sessions, there was no system in place within the Met to help me.

A lot of people who are prone to bulimia and anorexia are said to be perfectionist. And my life was far from perfect at that point. I was in trouble on a range of fronts, and in some emotional pain. Bulimia is a response to suffering, and life is never totally free of that. But it's not a healthy way to deal with problems, internalising them and using the cycle of overeating and vomiting as a release. In reality there was a lot to deal with and a lot that was wrong for me. I was in recovery from a major life-threatening experience, and partly as a consequence of this my marriage was going downhill fast. The door had opened on a new relationship with Barry, which started as the rollercoaster ride it would always be. On top of this I had nothing much outside the four walls of my home to distract me, no job with its status and demands, just the relative isolation of being at home with my young child. It was a wonderful opportunity to spend time with Ben, but nevertheless it was a huge adjustment.

As was the impending break-up of our marriage, for

which I felt I had to bear the major responsibility. I had initiated the split. Separation was not something that Pat had wanted at all. Around Christmas he moved out to live with his mum and dad. Harrowing as his departure was, it was a relief when he'd gone, though I was plagued with guilt about what I was doing. I'd been pretty horrible to him. I'd lost control and hadn't behaved well. He's a nice chap; it was a shame. Our divorce finally came through in early 1993. It was nerve-racking and far from easy. For a start, when I returned to Wood Green station in the late summer of 1992 it was only after Pat had been transferred from there to Enfield. The Met must have encountered a lot of this sort of professional/personal overlap, and they were accommodating. Pat, understandably, hadn't given in without a fight. He saw himself as the wounded one, but I was suffering too. And there was Ben to consider.

There were all sorts of arguments. What we fought about most was the fridge-freezer. It went on for months, but I won in the end. Looking back, it's quite funny, and these days we get along fine. For Pat, there was a happy ending sooner rather than later: he met someone else over Christmas that year, the same woman to whom he is now happily married.

In December Ben and I went on holiday for a week with Jeni Lawson. We spent the week in a villa in Portugal owned by a retired PC who had heard about the stabbing in the newspapers and wanted to help us out. He let us stay in his apartment rent free for the week. Jeni had organised it all, and it was marvellous that she did. It gave me a very welcome break at a very low point, and she was a good friend to me then, as she was to prove later.

Christmas was spent in Childswickham with Ben and

my parents. As the New Year dawned I felt totally demoralised. Ben's presence was a great help, because I had to look after him: I was his mum, which gave me a lot of emotional strength, but being a mum *and* a WPC again was tough. Once after a night of virtually no sleep because Ben was suffering from an ear infection I went to my GP. I was after a prescription for Ben, but when he saw the exhausted state I was in he wrote me a sick note. He told me I had to look after Ben. I was lucky that he was so perceptive and sympathetic. On the sickness certificate he cited my symptoms as trouble with my periods, using the technical term dysmenorrhoea, which he thought no one would understand anyway. He didn't mention stress. I told him that once that word got out you were done for. He was switched on to my problems with stress, but sensitive enough to realise the lack of credibility such a diagnosis would muster with the Met.

On the whole I felt completely useless. Physically I was stronger, but there was some way to go. My injuries, apart from my little finger, were healing. This weakness remained a constant reminder of what had happened, even now, several years later. The scar from the wound to my shoulder, which had gone into ridges, needed steroid injections. (It's never come quite right and I am still self-conscious about it to this day: I avoid exposing it.) Psychologically I was a bit of a mess, to say the least, and feeling vulnerable.

By this time Barry and I were half living together. He would stay with me for days at a time, but he never gave up his flat in nearby Enfield and never committed himself totally to me. The nearest he ever came to doing so was when he turned up one day with his microwave. I knew then that things were moving into a different gear. But when he took it back again a while later the message was equally clear. There was a funny side to it, as there always is, but then I was in a desperate frame of mind, and I'd come to rely on him. It wasn't fair of me, but when he told me that he and a friend had planned a three-week trip to Australia, New Zealand and Fiji that March I didn't want him to go. It was a very difficult time, because wise old Barry had always been there for me.

I felt bereft when he left for the other side of the world, even though it was only for three weeks. I felt my life support had gone. This may appear something of an over-dramatisation, but by then I had lost my sense of proportion as well as my sense of humour. I was also short on the wisdom stakes, which became clear when I attempted a reconciliation with Pat. I still felt guilty and distraught about the break-up of our marriage, so for what I thought were the best of reasons I tried to make a go of it with him again. This turned out to be a terrible mistake and a disaster. To cap it all, when he returned from his holiday, Barry wasn't best pleased to hear of it. I was sinking deeper and deeper into the mire that my life had become, betraying not only myself but also those closest to me.

It was at this point that I had the further disruption of having to leave the flat I'd shared with Pat because he wanted to let it. He was now living with his future wife and needed to raise funds, I recall, so I found a house to rent nearby and moved in during April 1992. I'd just got myself settled there with Ben, when a major distraction arrived in the shape of a return-to-work date. I had been to Wellington House, near New Scotland Yard, to see the CMO a few times over the months of my convalescence.

He was aware of what was happening to me and gave me more time off to recover. I suppose he knew more than I did of the psychological problems.

At some point that late spring I was considered well enough to return to light duties, for four hours a day. My start date was 25 May, and I was to help WPC Marion Macaskill, who had three years more service than me and worked as a collater on B-Relief. She is probably my closest friend and one of the other eight women on our relief of around forty officers. We'd got on right from the start, from when I was at Hornsey. I recognised Marion as like-minded. Our personalities are similar, and at heart we are both country girls, Marion coming from the wilds of Scotland. She was good at her job and well thought of, a real professional. I don't know what makes you like someone, but she was just a really nice person. Everyone liked her, and I was drawn to her too, not just because she was one of the few other women on the relief. The station is a very male world, but I didn't feel the need to link up with her because of her sex. Sometimes a few of us WPCs would all sit together at a table in the canteen, and there'd be a few jokes and remarks like, 'They're quite formidable when they get together.' We were quite intimidating to some of the men. It was rare for us to work together, though.

Nevertheless, I found myself working alongside Marion when I returned to light duties, based this time at Hornsey. Mr Camalletti, our detective chief inspector, had arranged this. I was grateful to him and found him one of the few who were helpful to me when I started back at the station that May. I was to remain on light duties from the end of May to mid-July. John Davison was among the supervising officers who wrote up my Annual Performance Appraisal

(APA) in September 1992, when I'd been back on full duties for just over a month and had been transferred back to Wood Green. He said that he was impressed by my positive attitude to my work and by the steps I had taken to regain my confidence. He felt that my recovery was largely due to my own strength of character.

I appreciated his faith in me. It was proving a struggle to believe in myself. On my first day back the Met didn't help me much on that score. In fact, what happened was quite damaging. Chief Superintendent Thornton was scheduled to meet me at a particular time at Hornsey station to welcome me back. Barry had seen the tears and the worry at home, how hard I was finding it to summon up the courage just to put my uniform back on, never mind returning to duty. It was a very big day for me and, even though it was something I wanted to do, I'd been living on my nerves for weeks. I wasn't after special treatment, just some acknowledgement and a sense that I had some support. When Thornton wasn't there, for an appointment I had been told to attend, I just thought, Well, that's how important I am.

Barry went berserk and hit the roof at Thornton's absence, explained later as attributable to something more pressing. Barry himself had been there for me for months, reassuring me that I'd make it through this bad patch and back to the work I had so enjoyed. He had given me the confidence to do so, but when I got there no one seemed to care. The Met's insensitivity didn't stop there. It took Barry to walk me down to the scene of the stabbing soon after I went back, albeit with the backing of our relief inspector, Bill Tillbrook, a kind, thoughtful man. He was switched on to what I needed. Why weren't they all? All it took was a walk around Wood Green with someone I trusted to hold my hand.

On one of my first days back on full duties I was out on patrol in a Panda around Wood Green when I noticed a couple of people in a car behaving suspiciously. I can't put my finger on exactly what it was I found odd about their behaviour — perhaps it was the old sixth sense at work again. I just knew it was a good stop. The car disappeared quickly down a side-street, and we set off in pursuit. As we turned off the main road, the car ahead pulled up to the kerb and parked a few hundred yards further on, and we saw two men get out and walk off in opposite directions. My colleague Dino Andrews went after one of them and managed to stop him fairly effortlessly, while I went after the other, an older man, a certain Shane Parker also known as Webster, who took to his heels as soon as he saw me. I rose to the challenge and ran after him, chasing him over back gardens and fences and keeping the control room at Hornsey informed on my PR. Eventually I was joined by the dog section, who arrested him in one of the several back gardens through which I'd scrambled. In the boot of their car we found computer equipment, which turned out to have been stolen from Essenden School in Hertfordshire. For our trouble we had an official thank you from the divisional commander of Hertfordshire Constabulary, Superintendent Reid, and I received a personal letter from one Superintendent Thornton, saying well done and complimenting me on an excellent arrest. I was also awarded a Chief Superintendent's Commendation for, as the gold-trimmed certificate headed with a heraldic ER declares, 'persistence and tenacity in the pursuit and arrest of a man for burglary'. But the greatest reward in my book was my immediate feeling of relief after the arrest. Thank God, I thought, I've still got it. I hadn't lost my touch. That was really pleasing.

Something that pleased me less was a call one day a while later to a flat in Hornsey. Haringey Council were trying to gain access for some reason, and as all the normal channels had failed they requested our assistance. What I realised as we were driving over there was that the thorn in the council's flesh was none other than the brother of Rupert West, who, like his sibling, had a history of violence. I began to feel uncomfortable and nervous as we got closer to the street in which he lived. But I was saved any further trauma because, luckily, he was out.

When Jeni Lawson returned to work shortly after I did, I made absolutely sure that she didn't receive the same neglectful treatment as I had on my first day back. The chief superintendent didn't forget about her. I knew how badly his absence on my first day back had affected me, and I was damned if Jeni was going to be slighted like that. But what I had no control over was how Jeni herself dealt with her return to the job. She never coped well from that day on. From December 1991 to June 1992 she was off sick. She returned to light duties for a period until she resumed full duties later that year, but she began to get a reputation for being unable to cope. In December she went off sick again until the following February. Then she came back once more to light duties. She had difficulty in resuming full duties, and between February 1993 and November 1993 it is all a grey area. Finally, she was referred to Gordon Turnbull, the psychiatrist at Ticehurst House Hospital, and saw him in January 1994.

Jeni felt very alone. It would have been easier, she once

told me, if she'd died, because she believed that then she would have been better cared for. And it would have been preferable, she felt, that her parents had not had to live through the aftermath of the stabbing and the subsequent difficulties of dealing with someone suffering from PTSD. She was referred to Ticehurst by CMO Dr Johnson. He was a friend of Gordon Turnbull, who was behind the PTSD management programme. Before that she had been, like me, left drifting. Very little was done for us. And it was dreadful what was said behind her back: it reinforced my resolve not to be like that. Shark-infested waters have nothing on some police canteens.

On one occasion, after we had both returned to work in 1992, I was out with Barry in a Panda when a call came through about a woman who had lost the plot in the streets around Bounds Green underground station. She was going berserk with two kitchen knives, slashing car tyres and threatening passers-by. We were nearby when the call came out, and I drove fast through the afternoon traffic to get there, horn blaring and blue light flashing. Here we go again, I thought. I had a touch of *déjà vu*.

When we reached the scene it was to find two PCs in the area car from Edmonton already on the case. The woman was in her fifties, of medium height, slim build and essentially nondescript. She obviously had a few connections loose but the kitchen knives were huge and she was brandishing them wildly, one in each hand. My stomach was in my mouth as we leapt out of the car.

The Edmonton PCs already had their truncheons drawn, and all four of us tried to keep our distance as we attempted to talk her into putting down the knives as she pranced around waving them and yelling abuse. She kept lunging at us, and we kept dodging out of the way, not keen to get within striking distance, though it became obvious that that was what we would have to do to disarm her. Eventually one of the Edmonton officers used his truncheon to strike her on the arm, and as he did so Barry and I, me at the front and Barry to one side, rugby-tackled her to the ground. She was immediately disarmed, handcuffed and put in the back of the van to be taken to Hornsey.

After we'd booked her in, Barry and I had a rapid debrief in one of the interview rooms. I felt all right, if a bit shaken up, but our short discussion somehow acknowledged what had happened and helped me to deal with it. It was tremendously supportive, as was he. After this it was just a matter of writing up our notes on the incident, for which we both later received a Chief Superintendent's Commendation.

When we had first got back to the station it was to find Jeni pacing up and down the passageway in an extremely agitated state. Although she hadn't been directly involved, she had nevertheless lived through it as if she had been out there with us. This shows how tough it can be, though my own anxieties after the stabbing were never dominated by the fear of being stabbed again. It affected me more subtly and less directly than that, as I'm sure it did Jeni too. From the day Rupert West stabbed her, she was never the same WPC. During the interview that the press conducted when we were side by side in our hospital beds, Jeni declared bravely, 'I wouldn't think of quitting. This could have happened to anybody. You always know there are dangers, but you get on with it.' After the trial she was marginally less optimistic as she commented on how the incident had damaged her professional confidence, as it had done for all of us. In a piece in the *Daily Telegraph* she said: 'It does knock you a little bit. You wonder about your own confidence and meeting strange people. You accept the risks and try to keep them in the back of your mind.'

But, sadly, she had not been able to keep them there. Physically she was scarred for life from five wounds to the stomach, left breast and shoulder. But Rupert West's knife harmed not only her body. Though she attended Ticehurst House Hospital's PTSD management programme, her marriage cracked under the strain, and then, in March 1995, she was retired from the service. The Met offered her no retraining or rehabilitation: she was just told to see pensions, and that was it. End of story. It's a hard world. Only the strong survive. And for the time being I was among them.

CHAPTER 7

THE BOMBING: AN IRA DOUBLE

There was a derelict, end-of-the-world feel about a place that, a fortnight before Christmas, would normally have been abuzz with festive shoppers. On the ground a thick carpet of glass lay like the snow we'd been expecting that December. Smoke hung in the air in the funereal pall of an early-morning ground fog, slowly rising above it. The IRA had just issued a second coded warning. Their target was a nearby pub, just up a few blocks from where I stood on a corner of the Wood Green High Road. The pub itself lay outside the police security line. They obviously knew where we had placed the cordon, or, at least, had made an educated guess. Or perhaps, most eerily, they were watching us.

A few moments earlier a bomb had exploded in a litter bin outside Wood Green Shopping City. Seconds before I'd been next to it. My mind was in a spin as I stood recovering a few blocks away, caught in a whirlpool of emotions, being dragged further and further down. All of a sudden I remembered something that made me surface abruptly. Ben was due to meet me soon. Earlier that morning I'd made an arrangement with my nanny Michelle to bring him to me when I finished early turn that afternoon. His Sunday school were giving a party for all the kids. I'd planned to go with them, and we were going to drive there together. It was possible that Michelle might have left early with Ben for a morning of Christmas shopping and a quick bite of lunch before our two o'clock rendezvous.

With that thought in mind I rushed across the road to a newsagent. They'd been in the thick of it too, but there was a sort of Dunkirk spirit about, a pervasive sense that we all had to muck in and help each other. No one, bar the IRA, knew what might happen next. My mind was racing: all I could focus on was that I had to stop them driving into this. And pray to God that they weren't already here. The idea that my precious little boy might be anywhere near this mayhem filled me with horror. My brain was awash with myriad possibilities as I rushed up to the counter and, without pausing for breath, explained my problem. The Asian shopkeeper ushered me quickly into a back room and in seconds I found myself talking to Michelle. Relief washed over me when I heard her voice. It wasn't often that home and work overlapped. And thank God for that. There I was in the middle of a terrorist bomb scare — not just a scare either — with my own safety in severe jeopardy, having to worry about my two-year-old. It was all too much.

Had I but known it, it had been for some time. Women in general were under-represented in the higher echelons of the force: there was one female inspector on another relief, and there were a couple of female sergeants, one of whom had children, but worked part-time. As things stand in the Met, according to the Commissioner's Annual Report for 1998/9 there are just two women who have reached the rank category of commissioner or assistant commissioner, or their deputies, though increasing numbers of female officers are making it into the managerial roles of sergeant and above. There are 2 women among 26 commanders, 9 among 227 superintendents, 16 among 369 chief inspectors, 56 among 1,205 inspectors and 386 among 4,323 sergeants. But in a workforce of which even today only some 17 per cent of constables are women, and women in the rank of sergeant and above constitute less than 8 per cent, I'm pretty sure that it's still rare in the Met to find women with children in high-up positions.

Because none of the other WPCs with whom I worked had kids, no one had any real idea of the amount of juggling involved in my life. At that time no one, except Barry, ever saw the reality. My parents lived a long way away and, though they always came to my aid at times of crisis, they just didn't realise the day-to-day struggle I went through to keep things together. Why should they? I was never a whinger, and we were always encouraged as kids to put up and shut up. If you can't stand the heat, stay out of the kitchen. The fact was that they were busy people with their own lives, both of them still working, and we'd never been ones for cosy heart-to-hearts. They were always there for me when I needed them, but I never took advantage. When things got tough I'd mostly just grin and bear it. I was famous for my resilient, beaming smile.

Most of my friends were in the police force, and we never discussed its pressures much either. Frankly, there was little point. And I wanted to make the best of it. At the end of the day nobody ever said much, or came anywhere near to suggesting that I might have got out of my depth. No one dared to say that my work with the Met was not suitable for a single woman with a young child. I wouldn't have encouraged it: it was not an image I projected of myself. I was a tough, capable policewoman: tough in that I was super-fit, tough in that I didn't mind getting involved in fights. I wasn't at all worried about any of that. That wasn't something you could worry about and do the job; it just wasn't part of me or the police culture in which, at least outwardly, I thrived. Of course, now I'm very different. These days I would feel uncomfortable and unhappy about doing anything if I didn't feel safe. Then, I just walked towards danger with the best of them.

On the day of the bombing I was on early turn, which meant that Michelle had to arrive at my home in Cheshunt at five in the morning for me to leave the house in time for a six o'clock start. How many nannies would arrive at 5 a.m. to begin a day's work? But Michelle was extremely accommodating, and I knew only too well how incredibly fortunate I was to have found her.

Childcare had been a perpetual problem from day one and eventually became a nightmare headache. To begin with Pat and I had employed the wife of a colleague. It was the first time she had tried her hand at child-minding, and after a few weeks I think she realised it wasn't really her cup of tea. Pat had taken the job of crime prevention officer to fit in with my shift work, which meant that Ben spent as little time as possible with the child-minder. But that arrangement ceased around the time of the stabbing, after which I was with Ben until I went back to work. Then, of course, when I separated from Pat I had to make other arrangements.

It was at this point, May 1992, that Michelle arrived. She'd placed an ad in a local newspaper, and I went to interview her at the home in Hoddesdon she shared with her parents. I explained that the hours would have to be flexible enough to cover my shifts, and this didn't put her off. The only drawback for me was that Michelle didn't own a car, so sometimes I had to lend her mine, which meant that I was dependent on Barry to get me from Cheshunt to Wood Green. If he wasn't staying with me, he would drive over from his flat in Enfield to pick me up for work. Early turns, late turns, nights. I was lucky that he was willing and able to help out, otherwise I don't know what I would have done. I was already spending half my salary on rent, and the cost of childcare added to that didn't leave me with much to live on. Without Barry's help there would have been more hassle and expense.

All this only emphasised even more to me, Ms Independent, how reliant I'd become on other people, and how isolated I felt without any close family living nearby to help me out. I was indebted to Barry but Michelle especially was crucial to the juggling act that my life had become. If she didn't turn up, I couldn't go to work as I had no one else to turn to. Fortunately I had struck gold with Michelle, but even with her invaluable support it was hard work and lonely, and made me feel quite vulnerable.

Everything had to fit in around my job, including my young son. Work was a lot of things to me, but at that moment the income I earned from it was vital. I spent my life whizzing around, I just had to do it all. When I look back, I don't know how on earth I managed. When I recall how many times I left Ben with au pairs I hardly knew I flinch. But at that time little Ben, so easy-going and adaptable, got along very well with Michelle, and with Barry, too, as it turned out.

Initially Barry was not so much wary of Ben as just not used to children. As a single man in his late twenties he had no experience of them. But he proved a natural and became very fond of my Ben. Ben and he had a fantastic relationship and spent a lot of time together. When I was studying for the first stage of the Met's sergeants' exams between mid-1992 and March 1993, Barry would take Ben out for a walk or to the park, out and about anywhere and everywhere, to give me the chance to study. Barry had brought round his old desk and chair, the furniture he'd used when he was working towards his sergeant's exams, and we'd set it up in a corner of my bedroom. Any spare time I'd be up there, and on days when I didn't want ever again to see another police-training manual Barry would always encourage me. He would pack me off to my room and take Ben out or entertain him indoors for hours at a time.

I studied with a passion, between shifts and training in the gym, between Ben and Barry. There was never a moment to myself. I have no idea now how I did it. I find it hard enough, these days, to fit everything in. Then I was just on the go all the time. Completely exhausted. That's how Barry remembers me: always tired.

But I was enjoying that heady mix of exhilaration edged with fear that goes with all the fun of the fair. My life was a rollercoaster ride. I'd scream and shout along with the best of them on the twists and turns of the track as it peaked and plunged. One day, though, it wasn't any longer for the joy of it: I wasn't waving but drowning. But how could they tell? For now no one, including me, knew any different, and I was determined to stay on until the end. The day of the bombing was no exception.

I'd arrived that morning in the cold and dark at six. There wasn't much happening and, as it was a quiet start to the day, I'd been relieved of my regular duties to do some studying. On days like this I often managed to slot in a couple of hours' work between half past six and nine o'clock, tucked away in one of the tiny overspill offices at the station. Barry used to pop in to see me from time to time to crack the whip and make sure I hadn't fallen asleep.

When I next glanced at my watch I was surprised to see that it was coming up to nine. Feeling virtuous, I piled up my books on a corner of the desk and headed across the station yard towards the canteen and breakfast. Although Wood Green police station itself is a reasonably attractive red-brick Victorian building, the canteen had no such appeal. It was basically a shed at the back of the station yard where all the police vehicles were parked. I was hungry that morning, so not overly concerned about my surroundings as I ordered my breakfast and looked around for a seat. It was a busy time and I had trouble finding one. I needn't have bothered, because I'd just sat down when the call came over the radio.

The morning's bustle and talk stopped abruptly. We all knew immediately what it meant. With barely a word and, as if invisibly joined at the hip, every officer in the canteen simultaneously got to their feet and left the building. Breakfasts lay abandoned on the formica tables as we raced into the yard and scrambled into all the available vehicles. About ten of us, a DI and a DCI included, climbed into one of the carriers, a Sherpa, which set off at speed towards the Shopping City. We had less than twenty minutes in which to evacuate the area. The IRA had planted a bomb there.

As I'd raced into the yard I saw Barry, custody officer that day, strolling purposefully towards the main station building with a cup of tea. He shot me an eyes-raised-skywards look that said it all: Here we go again. It's crazy, really, when you consider it logically, that you rush towards a place of danger. You're working against nature. Your instinct tells you to run away, to get the hell out of it, but your police training tells you to do the exact opposite. It's all part and parcel of the job to absorb the knocks, but the price this exacts is variable, though there is no escape: drink or divorce, wife-beating or over-training in the gym. The police service is full of this. Whoever you are and however macho you think you might be, the job has to catch up with you at some point. It might just snap at your ankles for years, or go for the jugular when you least expect it.

As we sped off down Wood Green High Road we had no idea of the exact location of the bomb or if there was more than one. The telephone warnings from the terrorists had been vague in most respects. Bomb or bombs were not our prime concern. We were the first team of officers at the scene, and the safety of the public had to be our priority. The carrier stopped about a hundred yards from the shopping centre, and we scattered in a kaleidoscope of directions. Our evacuation began with the local shops. Although we'd been told that the bomb was set to detonate at around 9.35 a.m., the location we'd been given, Wood Green Shopping City, was a vast space to cover and clear. And 9.35 a.m. was just about the time when a huge number of Christmas shoppers, with less than a fortnight's shopping days to go, were expected to flood into the area. The pressure was on.

The warning, using a codeword, had been phoned to the Associated Press news agency at 9.15 a.m. The journalist who took the message said that the caller had told him there were two large devices, and the police had twenty minutes to clear the area. We were running in and out of the shops as fast as we could, getting people out. An anti-terrorist source said later that the bombers knew the call was too late for the police to do anything.

The public can let you down sometimes. I got an earful of 'Oh, do we have to? We've come out for a morning's shopping, and you're inconveniencing us.' It's the sort of attitude I come up against a lot. I suppose if you cry wolf too often, people become blasé. But this wasn't anything to take lightly. It was no rehearsal.

I'd got as far as Argos and was darting round the store encouraging shoppers to leave. I headed towards the rear exit in order to take a short cut to the furniture shop next door. I just barked out the same thing over and over, but one old boy who worked there wasn't too bothered. He was taking it easy, as if priding himself on his ability to remain unruffled. He was talking to me as if we were exchanging pleasantries at a bus stop, cracking jokes as he made his way towards the cloakroom to retrieve his coat. I urged him to hurry. He took no notice and tried to distract me with some playful banter. We were the last out, and I watched with relief as he stepped on to the escalator to make his way to the ground floor and the exit. Nothing, especially a bomb scare, was going to cramp his style as he carried on with his jokey chat. Finally he got to the glass doors that led on to the covered walkway. He wasn't leaving without having the last word but as he turned to me ... There were no preliminary rumblings like you get in a thunderstorm, just a stark boom. It was as if he'd been trying to warn me.

The noise was deafening. It was the most massive explosion I'd ever heard and quite clear several miles distant. Barry certainly heard it as he form-filled in the station charge room. He feared for us, but what could he do? Even if he'd been there he could only have watched as the strength of the blast knocked me off my feet. A split-second before I went I caught the look of total horror on the face of the old boy from the furniture store. As long as I live I'll never forget that expression of naked fear. Afterwards there was a deathly silence broken only by the flutter of a hundred pigeons' wings and a rising chorus of security alarms. I got to my feet but could see little through the thick shroud of smoke. For a moment there was nothing to anchor me, no familiar landmarks with which to make sense of the world. I felt very afraid.

The jokey man was getting to his feet, no longer joking. He was walking away in a hurry, in silence, his humour suspended. I guessed it would take him a while to regain his irreverent slant on life. Physically unharmed, he was wobbly on his feet and clearly in shock. I followed him out on to the street to face a scene of total devastation. I pulled myself together sufficiently to encourage a few waifs and strays out of the immediate vicinity. I learnt later that the bomb had exploded in a dustbin outside W. H. Smith's, only twenty-five feet from where I'd been standing. It had gone off under the covered walkway, which contained but concentrated the blast, within ninety seconds of the beginning of our evacuation. Hardly the twenty minutes we'd been led to expect. It was only a pound of Semtex, but if that's a small bomb I never want to be around anything bigger. My colleague PC Scott Lewis had been right by the bin when it went off. He was lucky to escape with only a few cuts and bruises. He could have been killed. One of the other injured officers was nineteen-year-old probationer Ian Fenton who had begun work fresh from training that Monday. For him it was, as Chief Superintendent Hugh Thornton later described it, a baptism of fire.

A PC across the other side of the High Road had, like me, been knocked off his feet by the strength of the blast. I saw him struggling as I contemplated my next move. It was John Adams, who had shared another hellish moment with me in Wood Green when he'd come to our rescue at the stabbing. John was later awarded the MBE for his work within the Wood Green community but, like so many of us, he took early retirement on the grounds of ill-health, due to injuries incurred during his service.

Get the hell out. Run. My mind was racing out of there already. But I had a job to do. A man came tearing past me in a blind panic. He'd lost it completely and was hysterical, not willing or able to be reasoned with. There was nothing I could do to stop him as he pushed his way through the doors from which I'd just emerged. I chased after him, urging him to come back, but he just ignored me and carried on running. I had too much else to do to focus on just one person, so I let him go.

As I began to get my bearings I noticed WPC Sharon Kenyon from my relief standing outside Argos. She looked rooted to the spot. I called over to her, and we both set off at a run in the direction of Wood Green underground station. I remember saying, 'This fucking job!' I wasn't joking. Day to day it was bad enough, even though there is the reward that you know you're doing a good job. But no one knows what's involved. No one knows the daily dangers. No one knows the price we pay. No one knows, unless they've done it, what it's like to walk down the street in a police uniform and be immediately identifiable and hated by certain sections of the community who would do you harm. That was hard enough, but ordinary enough. Now, too, there was this with which to contend.

I felt exposed and vulnerable. We were standing on shifting sands and hadn't a clue where the ground would next give way. No idea from which bit of the sky something might fall and harm us. As we jogged through the litter of metal signposts felled like trees, bits of building, concrete and glass, metal and brick, thrown about like toys, we didn't know what else to do but continue to clear the area. Exactly five minutes after the first and exactly where Sharon had been standing, just moments earlier, a second bomb went off. Rosemarie Brown, the manager of W. H. Smith's that day, had still been inside her store when the first bomb exploded, and had just got out when the second went off in a bin in the street outside Argos. As the ground shook beneath me I could only thank my lucky stars that we hadn't hung around. We were still as close as anyone to that second bomb.

Now it was time to think about our own safety. With the area clear, we headed towards the carrier, parked as a makeshift roadblock at an angle across Wood Green High Road. Scott was in severe shock, as were most of us. One of the WPCs was in tears. Mitch, our driver, turned the Sherpa round and drove up the road away from the epicentre of the blasts. By this time there was a proper cordon across the road and more police in attendance, brought in from all over Hornsey Division. We ten from Wood Green had been the first officers at the scene and the only ones there when the first bomb went off.

The carrier stopped suddenly, and we took this as our cue to jump out again and get on with our evacuation of the surrounding shops and streets. By this time any niceties had vanished and I just screamed at people to go. Clear off. I could be aggressive when I wanted and now was no time to hold back.

There'd been a second bomb, there could well be a third. Sure enough, within minutes there was another call from the IRA: a warning about a bomb in a pub. This turned out to be a hoax, but a more deeply unpleasant one I can hardly imagine — presumably all part of the plan to cause maximum disruption to daily life in the capital. And it worked. Less than twenty-four hours earlier, and only a few miles from Wood Green, an IRA car bomb outside Woodside Park tube station in North Finchley had brought chaos to commuters. The then Prime Minister John Major called for increased vigilance by the public in the run-up to Christmas and said that though the bombers hoped to gain political capital by their actions, they wouldn't. The week before, two bombs had exploded in Manchester city centre, injuring more than sixty people and causing an estimated loss of £3 million in trade and damage to buildings. These bombs in Wood Green were the latest attacks in the most intensive IRA campaign on the mainland since the 1970s. The ripples from the blasts reached far and wide, not the least of it affecting the transport system, with all the major bus routes to and from the area, as well as all underground connections, in shutdown. No one was going anywhere in a hurry that day.

This was when I'd remembered Ben. After I'd made my call to Michelle, I felt a sense of relief wash over me. But my contact with the outside world had brought me back to reality and all of a sudden I began to feel shaky. I wanted to get the hell out of there. And, luckily, that is exactly what we did, leaving the police forensic officers to sift through the wreckage.

With any major incident such as this the procedure the Met follows is for higher-ranking officers to take immediate charge. Hence the presence of a DI and a DCI in our carrier from Wood Green station that morning, though DI Jones and DCI Camalletti were the type who would muck in whatever. But there was nothing special that either they or we could do. There was no magic wand to be waved to make things better. All we could do was what we did: evacuate the area as quickly as possible. Of course, there is the risk that if you don't know exactly where the bomb is planted you may take people towards it rather than away from it. By encouraging people out of the shops and on to the streets, although our ultimate aim had been to get them out of the area, we had taken them unwittingly right past the spot where both bombs were secreted.

Back in the station canteen Sharon and I sat at a table. After a while she began to cry. I didn't blame her. What we'd just been through was horrendous. Unlike her, though, I didn't, simply couldn't, display my feelings so publicly. I just leant forward on the table and cradled my head in my arms. When I'd recovered enough I put my energies into comforting Sharon. The fact was that, although most of us had tried to cover up our emotions, we all felt the same and hung around together in the canteen, drinking cups of hot sweet tea.

As usual, Barry was switched on to what was needed. He was only too aware of the effect such incidents can have. He did what he could within the limits of what was available to him and contacted Welfare and the police surgeon. Mick Simms, of Welfare, came to the station that afternoon, preceded by the police doctor who gave each of us a quick check-up. In all, ten people were hurt that morning by flying glass, including Scott, and two other PCs. It was only luck that no one had been more seriously hurt or killed. Scott was taken to the North Middlesex, the hospital where I had been just fifteen months earlier. Those terrorist bombs had exploded only yards from the spot on which Rupert West had knifed me.

Barry had organised a short debriefing session, which involved a group of us sitting down together in one room to go over the events of the morning: where we'd been, what we'd seen and what we'd done. There was nothing specially planned, intense or mysterious about it. We all just said what we felt we had to say, anything that would help us through it. As far as counselling went, this was it. Then there was nothing else to do but go home.

The following day the *Daily Mail* described me as a 'Heroine PC'. I didn't feel much like one. All I knew was that my head ached, and there was a steady ringing in my ears. Later I discovered a few bruises, and that was it. Ben and I never did make it to the Sunday school party. I was due for a long weekend off that Friday through Sunday, and Barry and I had been planning to visit my mum and dad in Worcestershire. We went to Cheshunt to pick up Ben and stuck to our arrangement. Barry drove us there. I was still in a state of shock and very withdrawn. Barry was finding it difficult to face yet another big problem in my life, to deal with the turmoil it introduced into our relationship. This time he was involved both personally and professionally, and he found it impossible to help me because he was so caught up in it. He felt he could take on everything himself, that he could deal with all that was thrown at us without any outside help. He was very proud. He saw his job as to protect me and guide me in the right direction again, to put me back on track.

The Wood Green bombs were a watershed for us. It was then that Barry began to realise he couldn't make things better, not for me, not for himself and not for us. There were too many variables. I didn't live in a cocoon of cotton wool. I lived in the real world. I did a dangerous job. I

could have died in the IRA bombing in Wood Green
Shopping City, like WPC Jane Arbuthnott had in December
1983, the year before I joined the Cadets. On the Saturday
afternoon before that Christmas the London Samaritans
had received a phone call from a man with an Irish accent
who used a code word known only to the police and the
IRA. In it he warned that car bombs had been planted
outside Harrods, with more bombs inside the store and
another at Littlewoods in Oxford Street. When she went to
investigate a car parked outside Harrods the vehicle
exploded, and Jane Arbuthnott was killed outright.

My latest narrow escape had taken its toll on Barry. By
the time we split up later the following year I swear that he
was showing many of the symptoms of PTSD. He
eventually dealt with it that weekend by running away,
something people often do, and he drove back to London
on his own, leaving me and Ben in Childswickham without
a car. I put all my anger towards him into that. There I
was, stuck in the middle of nowhere without any means of
transport. But my true distress was at finding myself
without him and his emotional support.

In Worcestershire my father had heard about the
bombing from a neighbour, who had seen it on the TV
news. Poor Dad, I can only imagine how he felt, learning
about it second-hand like that. But over the years he had
been forced to adapt. It wasn't only me who had had such
close shaves with death: my brother, Peter, had been
involved in a serious motorbike accident in the mid-eighties
and was fortunate to have come out of it alive. Later, after
the shooting, friends and neighbours came up to my parents
to express their concern at what they saw as our collective
misfortune as a family: 'You're so unlucky,' they'd say.

My mother's response was positive, even after all she'd been through: 'No, we are lucky, because she has survived.'

Immediately after the bombing the press got on to me again, just like after the stabbing. They'd even managed to get hold of my parents' phone number. Fortunately my mother was willing to field the calls. In fact, she was a pillar of strength throughout it all, and I can never thank her enough. The story appeared later in the *Gloucestershire Echo* with the headline, 'PC In Bomb Blast Drama', and it went on a bit about the stabbing. It was just a straightforward news piece about another major trauma in my life. But I couldn't really acknowledge its effects because I hadn't dealt with what had happened the first time. I knew, though, that I needed some time to recover, and the next week I returned to Cheshunt to see my GP. My mother drove me there and back again when he gave me a month off sick. There was no mention of stress on the sick note. I knew the rules. I wasn't going to be dismissed as a weakling. Instead I wanted to deny what had happened and lose myself in my studies.

The only person from senior management who contacted me during those four weeks off was DCI Camalletti. In all the years I knew him he never once let me down in my initial estimation of him as a lovely, caring person. He rang me in Worcestershire, where I stayed throughout my convalescence. When my mum took the call he asked her to tell me that if there was anything he could do for me that I shouldn't hesitate to phone him at home. Everyone used to pull my leg at work that he fancied me. Well, all I can say is that if you can't be kind to someone without having that levelled at you, then there's something wrong with the world.

As far as I am aware Mr Camalletti was just a thoughtful man who could use his imagination and put himself in someone else's shoes. Apart from his kindness there was not one thank-you or well-done from anyone else senior on Hornsey Division. If I had been hoping for any word of thanks for our work that day, I'd have had a long wait. None was ever forthcoming. There was not even any comment, good or bad, about it on my work report. Our role in what happened that day was never acknowledged and appeared simply forgotten. We were just doing our job.

Down in the peace and quiet of Worcestershire, I took only a couple of days off from studying. I saw the next month as the perfect opportunity to study hard. There was no pampering for me. No dwelling on what had happened. No wallowing. The first part of my sergeant's exams was less than three months away, and I knew that I had to work like crazy to pass. For a long time, then and later, whenever my mum asked Ben, 'Where's Mummy?' He would reply, 'Studying,' with all the solemnity of a two-year-old struggling with a big word that he didn't really understand. Ben and I spent Christmas in Childswickham with my parents. I made it as happy as I could for him, and my parents were wonderful as usual. Barry stayed with us until the Christmas morning, returning to London in the afternoon to spend the rest of the festive period with his mother. It was another estranged time. He was difficult and moody. I only had to say one thing wrong, and he'd be off and back to his flat. Apart from his moodiness, he was, like me, fiercely independent. Although we had been a couple, of sorts, for more than a year by then, our Christmas presents that year were bought and given separately.

Just before I went back to work I returned to Cheshunt. One afternoon a colleague, Paul Storey, came round to the house for a cup of tea. He was a lovely man who worked with both Barry and me, and I liked him very much. Something must have emboldened him because all of a sudden he said, 'You can't carry on like this. Apart from anything else it will destroy your relationship with Barry. It's all too close. Haven't you given enough?' He went on to mention that a vacancy had been advertised for a collater at Wood Green, a station-based job that involved building up a card-system databank on criminals. He suggested I might apply for what seemed like a worthwhile job. At first I was a bit taken aback, though I appreciated his frankness. Of course, I knew in my heart that he was probably right, but his advice fell on deaf ears. I realised I never would or could do anything like that. In my book an office job would have been a cop-out.

By the end of January 1993 I was back at work. Two months later, I passed the first part of the sergeants' exams. Not long after that I was contacted by some department from within the Met's labyrinthine administration system about an award I was to receive for my role in the stabbing. This was a police award for which I had been put forward by some of the senior management at Hornsey. In the letter I received from them, I was invited to go and collect my award, the Commissioner's Commendation, at a special presentation ceremony in New Scotland Yard. 'No, thanks,' I replied, 'just send it though the post.' I didn't want to rake over old coals. I didn't want any fuss. I just wanted to get on with my life and put it all behind me. But I have to admit that there was another reason too.

Senior management at Hornsey had recommended all

four of us for the Commissioner's Commendation for our roles in events leading up to the stabbing. They'd decided to recommend John Davison for the more prestigious Commissioner's High Commendation. Apart from not wanting to drag up the past, I felt reluctant to attend a presentation ceremony that in any way diminished what I had done that day. We had all four of us been there, and it just seemed wrong that John should have been put up for a higher award than the rest of us. No one else knew what had gone on. They hadn't been there. How could they assess the importance of what we'd done and rank us accordingly? As far as I was concerned no one's input was any more or less important than anyone else's. Except, of course, that John was a male sergeant, and we were female constables.

We had all done something at the scene that made up the final jigsaw of events. OK, John had talked West into handing over the knife. This undoubtedly took courage, but it had been no less or more vital than our equal contributions. It wasn't that I thought I was any better than anyone else, it was simply that I felt these senior managers had no right to sit in judgement over what had happened that day and thereby change its reality. This was something personal that they were trying to colonise. By offering John the higher award it was as if they were saying that we three women hadn't quite pulled our weight, or had pulled less weight. There was an assumption that getting the knife from West was something more crucial than what we, the three WPCs, had done.

But life is more organic than that, and to be brave doesn't necessarily mean doing something that fits in with the macho image of what bravery means. Surely there are many ways to be brave, not just the kung-fu way. And these gradations of the Commissioner's Commendation did not take account of this. I wouldn't want it said that I am taking anything away from John, but the fact is that someone tried to take something away from me. I couldn't see the point of making that distinction about our roles that day. It didn't make any sense to me. Why do it?

To get even a Commissioner's Commendation is considered a great honour, so my refusal to appear in person to receive the award was something of a snub. It wasn't the done thing, but it was what I wanted to do. I'd made my point. A year later, in 1994, I was awarded the Queen's Commendation for Brave Conduct. This is a civilian award, and we all received the same category of honour.

CHAPTER 8

CLIMBING THE RANKS AND FALLING APART

It was a routine police inquiry — aren't they all? — and dark outside when DS Bob Window knocked on the door of a house in Tottenham. When it opened he was greeted by a man holding a samurai sword. DS Window had gone to interview him in connection with an investigation he was conducting. He might well have been there to arrest him, though the details escape me. But whatever DS Window wanted that night, the man in question wasn't having it. In the fight that ensued DS Window lost a hand. It was cut off cleanly at the wrist.

We were out on patrol that night and accepted the call that followed. I was driving the van, Yankee Delta 2, and even though it wasn't on our ground we went along anyway to provide back-up. By the time we arrived DS Window was in extreme shock, pain and distress. All we could do while awaiting the ambulance was to go door to door to find as much ice — cubes, frozen food, anything — as we could to pack around the hand to keep it cold and slow degeneration. There was no time to dwell on the horror of it. We did what we could to make things better for the injured DS. When the air ambulance arrived he was flown to hospital where, thankfully, his hand was saved. DS Window is still with the Met, though I am not sure in what capacity. I imagine the incident was not an easy one with which to come to terms. After my encounter with Rupert West I could never stay away from sharp instruments. It was stressful enough to be a victim, but reminders were constant, triggering the memories, though it wasn't all as direct as kitchen knives and samurai swords.

One night near Turnpike Lane we did a stop on a Mini. When it pulled up at the side of the road we found ourselves face to face with a notorious bunch of self-styled gangsters, with a string of convictions for a range of crimes from deception to robbery. There was a good reason for the stop that particular night, which escapes me now, but it was backed up by our knowledge that most of the occupants of the car had criminal records as long as your arm. To begin with they used the standard ploy of making a scene and hoping that we'd give up and go away. What they hadn't reckoned on was our tenacity. Our relief was famous for it. We would rarely back down and drive off.

There used to be a joke when we were kids: How many elephants can you get in a Mini? Two in the front and two in the back was the answer, and it was as hard to extract those men from that car as it would have been for any elephant to have squeezed its way in. We were reduced to dragging them out bodily every which way, even through the sunroof. A car window was broken in the fight that ensued. When they still wouldn't budge I found myself leaning my head and upper body into the hornets' nest that the inside of the car had become. I could see that one of my collegues was struggling to extract the driver, who was still wearing his seatbelt, and we'd have been there all night otherwise. The reward for our perseverance was, among other things, a haul of stolen credit cards. I don't remember the details, but the suspects all got off later in court. Then they made a complaint against us. I've only recently discovered that the civil action against the commissioner has been dropped.

Another dark night I chased a burglar over a series of garden fences. Every week there was something. Before I met Rupert West or fell foul of the IRA's bomb offensive, there were scores of relatively minor incidents like these in which I put myself daily at risk. It wasn't a case of behaving like Super WPC, just that mostly I had to get on with the job in hand with only a cursory nod towards my own safety. You couldn't be foolhardy, that would be pointless and ridiculous, but when something had to be done, you had to do it. That was my approach. It did not cross my mind the time I chased the man who ran off as I was questioning him that he might be armed. Later I discovered he was wanted for armed robbery. On that occasion he was not carrying a gun. Of course, had I seen a weapon I should have got out of the way. But if it were a question of leaving others at risk, then I would have had to use what is called reasonable force to disarm him. You had to battle on, though there was always the risk that you might not survive the war.

One close shave came during the summer of 1993, shortly before I applied for the Armed Response Vehicles (ARV). I was out driving a Panda with a young probationer as my operator, and it was coming near to the end of our shift. We were late turn, two till ten, and it was dark. I guess we were drifting back towards the station when I first spotted the car, an old souped-up black Mini Metro kitted out with sports wheels and the like. My sixth sense was at work again, because something just didn't look right. The Metro disappeared up a side street into a road just off our ground. I followed. Strictly speaking this was Edmonton's patrol, and we were on the boundary where it met Hornsey. I flashed for the car to stop, which it did just up the street.

Inside there were four young black men. I got out of the Panda and went to speak to one of the passengers, while my colleague interviewed the driver. As the young man I'd approached opened the passenger door I noticed his distinctively long black-leather coat. It looked odd because it was unseasonably warm for the time of year. As a concession to this, he was wearing it unbuttoned. This enabled me to glimpse something heavy in the inside pocket, weighing it down. My eye caught a flash of metal. It looked like a gun.

My suspect was out on the pavement now, and he was big. I tried to wedge him between the car body and the door to stop him going anywhere, but he wasn't having it. He pushed past me, forcing me out of the way, and ran towards a house. As he did so someone opened the front door, and he slipped inside. He was followed by his mates. As rapidly as the door had opened it slammed in our faces. By the time we managed to get in, all our suspects had left by the back door.

We'd called for urgent assistance. But as we were on the divisional boundary no one could locate us. As I'd mentioned a gun, when help arrived it did so in the form of an ARV to back up the regular patrol car. One half of the ARV unit was PC Steve Dempsey, now my husband, who had accepted a call to the Rupert West knife attack two years earlier. Before long the scene was filled with police officers, Barry among them. In the house I had arrested a man and had him in quickcuffs, a particularly effective American import: they were rigid in the centre and allowed you to put painful pressure on the radial and ulnar nerves. No one struggled much in those: in fact, most people became quite compliant. Later I discovered that I had gripped the handcuffs so hard through fear and tension that to this day I am left with a dead spot on my thumb.

The man with the gun had gone, but not for long. A few streets away he met up with a couple of officers who had answered our call. They recognised him from my description and brought him back to the house for me to identify. He was still wearing that coat. But one thing was missing: the gun. Unless I had been very much mistaken, he had disposed of it. There was nothing more we could do so we went back to Wood Green with the prisoner. I was still there, processing the paperwork in the station office by the charge room, when the ARV unit of Steve and his co-operator, PC Chris Bishop, turned up. I'd been right about the gun. Although they were not authorised to search the house, Steve and Chris, with some help from the dog squad, had found a sawn-off shotgun in the back garden. Though later it could not be linked to the suspects, they had it with them in a black plastic bag. They pulled it out in front of me to take a closer look. Oh, by the way, they informed me casually, it's loaded.

My jaw almost hit the floor. I sank into a chair and couldn't move for a while. I knew the damage a sawn-off shotgun could cause. And I had been within inches of it. My life flashed before me, and not for the first time. For those first ten minutes at the scene, before the ARV unit and the other teams had arrived, we'd been easy targets, sitting ducks, completely on our own, exposed and vulnerable to whatever madness might have prevailed. It was a pretty shocking realisation to add to an already alarming night's work. In the end there was no resolution to the case, and none of the men was ever charged. I suspect it was all drugs-related, because it was commonly known that they were suppliers. The investigation was taken out of my hands and dealt with by CID, but no one could pin anything on them. In any case I later received a Chief Superintendent's Commendation for my work that night. I feel I deserved it. When I'd eventually got home I hadn't been able to sleep, so I'd called Barry. He'd come round to my flat, and we'd sat and talked late into the night. But there was no resolution for me either.

I was finding myself increasingly on my own now. Marion was always there for me, and I leant heavily on her friendship. If nothing needed saying, she wouldn't say it; if it needed saying, she said it; if I just needed her to listen, she listened. She got the balance right, which is quite an art and quite rare.

My relationship with Barry was under severe strain. As usual he had given me the belief in myself that I could qualify as a sergeant, and I passed my part one in the March. For the first exam Barry drove me up to Hendon to sit the written paper. Michelle had Ben for the day. Half-way through I had a panic attack, and my mind went blank. I couldn't remember a thing. It was quite a significant moment, and the first time anything like that had happened to me. I'm sure now that it was linked to the traumas I'd been through, that somehow it was a throwback to the effects of the knife attack. It was a dreadful feeling, but somehow I managed to pull myself out of it to finish the paper by the skin of my teeth.

Although I passed my part one, which was a huge relief, it was still not all plain sailing. I was overstretched financially, struggling to pay the high rent on the house in Cheshunt and to fund a full-time nanny, which together cost me the best part of a thousand pounds a month. Barry would help out with the odd bill, but I couldn't go on like that. It was quite an isolated time for me. I didn't do much more than work and study, train and look after Ben. There wasn't any time left for anything else. There are only so many hours in the day. I remember one afternoon I took a walk over to the park with Ben. It was an early spring day just before the first exam, and the point at which I realised that what I didn't know wasn't worth knowing. We spent a perfectly ordinary hour in the park: Ben and I had an ice cream, and he played on the swings, the usual things. It was the first time I'd done this for months, and it was such a treat. I'd been so tunnel-visioned on work and studying I was that easy to please.

I like my own company and know the people I like, but I am not particularly sociable. Neither is Barry, though if it came to it I think I have the edge. Sunday lunch at his mum's would be the social event of our week. Though I was very cut off I didn't think a lot about how I felt, especially as I'd channelled so much of my energy into working for the sergeants' exams. There's not a lot of time for introspection when you have a head full of Acts and Sections. Barry noticed that I was constantly tired and not able to concentrate. He had to badger me a lot to convince me to keep on studying. We had many an argument about that. I suppose I was very aware that I needed Barry, even though our relationship was so up and down. He alone seemed to understand how I felt and what I was going through, partly because of the sort of person he is, and partly because, like me, he was a police officer. But this was not the ideal ground on which to build a thriving relationship.

In the April we went on holiday to Canada for a couple of weeks. Barry organised it and paid for it, and it was a fantastic trip. We toured Nova Scotia in a hire car and drove along the East Canadian peninsula between the Gulf of St Lawrence and the Bay of Fundy. Ben stayed with my parents, because I didn't think that being on the road so much was a suitable vacation for a two-year-old. My family were glad to have him and, besides, I needed some time to myself and to spend on my own with Barry. Away from it all, mostly the pressure of work, we got along well.

You take yourself with you on holiday, and you bring yourself back, and the reality to which I returned was resonant with unresolved trauma. I had adapted superficially, but I had never made a true adjustment. I needed to appear strong and healthy, and I polished this image of myself as hard as I'd bulled my shoes when I was a cadet. My success in maintaining it was restricted to my work, where I was seen as an achiever who had overcome all obstacles. I'd made it through the written segment of the sergeants' exams, and ahead of me was part two, the practicals. I took these in October 1993 and passed. I was on my way to becoming one of the 10 per cent of uniformed women officers who are sergeants in the Met. It was now full steam ahead for the final stage: part three, a board assessment for which I awaited an interview date.

While I was climbing the ranks at work, at home I was falling apart. The image that reflected back at me there was cracked. Among other things, the rent on the Cheshunt house was crippling me financially, and I was finding it harder and harder to manage each month. Barry helped me to approach Welfare about this, and I got an appointment with Mick Simms, whom I'd seen twice briefly, after the stabbing and the bombs. He was extremely co-operative, and that May he got me into a three-bedroom ground-floor flat in a block in Enfield that was normally reserved for married officers. It was a huge relief. I lost my rent allowance, because the accommodation was paid for by the Met, but I came out of it £200 a month better off, which was welcome. Barry, Michelle and her boyfriend all helped me to redecorate and carpet the flat.

I was in by the end of May. But I never made it mine any more than I had made any of my other flats or houses into comfortable, attractive places in which to unwind at the end of a shift. They were always spotlessly clean, like my uniform, but I never really lived there. I didn't have any of the bits and pieces that make a house a home. I needed to provide a roof over our heads, and Ben never wanted for anything, but for me home was just a refuelling stop for what really mattered in life: my career as a police officer.

Michelle was still my nanny, and she came with me from Cheshunt to Culloden Road. However, by the end of that year she had decided it was time for her to move on. This was a great loss, because she was a lovely woman, Ben liked her, and she was a great asset to the smooth running of our household. I got through the nannies after that. To begin with, a couple who had a little boy of an age similar to Ben helped me out. They lived in an adjacent flat, and the husband was a policeman, so they understood about the vagaries of the job and of shift work. They took Ben in when I was at work. If I was on late turn Ben would stay with them and go to bed in their flat. When I got home at around ten thirty I would go and get him, bring him home and put him straight back to bed in our flat. On early turn Ben stayed the night with them. I wasn't really happy about any of this, because it was too unsettling for Ben, being traipsed around and woken up at night. It was quite a performance. I can't believe now some of the things I did. But I felt I had no choice.

Next I tried the au pair route. Françoise was French. She was with us in the summer of 1994, and she ran up a phone bill of £350 when I was away on my advanced driving course at Hendon. She had been making lengthy long-distance calls to France. I discovered this one night and left her a note to say we needed to talk. She must have found it the next morning, but I don't know because I never saw her again. When I got home late the following night she had disappeared back to France. Fortunately Ben was at my parents' that week, so I wasn't left in the lurch. After that I got call-barring.

I'd found Françoise through an agency. Through them I also discovered Gerry, the Australian. I didn't ask any of my au pairs to do much other than look after Ben when I wasn't there, but this girl was lazy, and we didn't hit it off. My main objection was that I felt she wasn't good with Ben. She also had little or no involvement with the job, evidenced by her departure the minute I walked through the door. We used to pass in the corridor like ships in the night. I took over the minute I got back from work, so I never had a moment to myself. I even took Ben with me when I went to train in the gym, the David Lloyd Centre in Enfield, where, fortunately, there was a crèche. It wasn't an easy existence.

At some stage I employed a very nice New Zealander. She was a great find. As well as being good with Ben, she was sweet to me, even cooking me meals in the evenings after work. She didn't last long, though, because she was in the middle of her round-the-world tour with London just a step on the way. And so it went on. I guess my mother was right when she used to say, 'What you really need, Helen, is a wife.'

It was Marilyn who was around when I was shot in late 1994. She had replaced Françoise, and, like her, was French. She was kind and nice with Ben, and the only drawback with her was that her English was poor. It wasn't too much of a problem, though, as Marion, who was often around at the time, would translate. Her French was a lot better than mine, and that helped enormously. Marilyn stayed with me for a while after the shooting when she returned from France to Enfield after the Christmas holidays, but by then I wasn't working so I couldn't justify keeping her. She went home early in 1995. That was when my life really turned into a bumpy ride, though this had nothing to do with looking after my son.

I'd got through four au pairs as well as my child-minding neighbours in the space of a year. Ben, as ever, was a credit to himself and never any trouble. I am really grateful to him that he's the type of kid he is. He has suffered from eczema since he was born, which can be a nervous condition, but apart from that he has shown no signs of distress in response to all the disruption. Someone who had poured oil on troubled waters was Barry, because Ben got along so well with him. That made any break with him hard. I had not only my own feelings to consider but also Ben's. Ben had known Barry since he was less than a year old, and Barry was around for the next two years. They were close, and Barry was there for him a lot of the time. That tied us all into a great big love knot that I found hard to undo when things went wrong. But it had to be done and, towards the end of 1993, Barry and I finally drifted apart. I was demanding and difficult, so Barry was moody and touchy. I only had to tut or sigh or make the wrong comment, and he'd be off. Towards the end we would wrong-foot each other constantly. He moved in and out, and it was a difficult and painful time. When he took back his alarm clock around Christmas of that year I knew that that was it.

The more I look back the more I realise how happy I am now, how my life has changed, how lucky I am to have found Steve. It was so horrendous then, but I never really thought about it like that. I just trundled on regardless. When the going gets tough, the tough get going. In that respect I am a typical Taurean, and the tougher it got the more my head went down. I charged at my life like the proverbial bull in a china shop. It was as if I had no regard for myself. It didn't matter how things were affecting me as a person, I was concerned only with driving myself, making myself continue along a route on which the inner me, the real me, had got left behind. My work as a police officer meant everything to me. It was my uniform that held me together and my career that maintained a structure to my life. But the foundations were not strong, and I was building something rickety and vulnerable to collapse at the least provocation. The edifice I had created was untenable. What I had soon to face was the harsh truth that I needed to knock the house down and start again. I began to feel that all that was left of me was an empty shell. That I had to get tougher and stronger to cope with what life threw at me when in truth I was just becoming more brittle. Any moment I might crack up. But I was determined not to. I would only crack on.

After each trauma my migraines had got progressively

worse. My periods stopped. I suffered from throat infections. My hair was falling out. The asthma, from which I had suffered mildly as a child, became more acute immediately after the stabbing and the bombings. Gradually I was beginning to suffer chronic physical symptoms from a build-up of stress. I was grinding my teeth at night and would wake up really tired each morning. I was always in tears, always arguing with Barry, lashing out at him, overwhelmed by the frustration I felt. At work I was a mature adult who could make life-or-death decisions, at home a five-year-old child who threw her teddy in a corner. I didn't understand what was happening or why I felt like that. Everything had got on top of me. I had allowed myself no space. And there was no security with Barry either. He would never commit himself. I was always frightened to say the wrong thing in case he packed his bag and moved out. I loved him, but I couldn't make the relationship work.

Towards the end of 1993 I did an instructors' course in self-defence, a two-week stint that would enable me to teach other officers and members of the public how best to protect themselves. I'd seen it advertised in *Police Orders*, a weekly internal newsheet that gave details of training opportunities and jobs. I signed up for it, and the Met paid. I had a particular goal in mind.

In late November I had joined the Shop Squad, a specialist team that worked at Wood Green Shopping City and dealt only with shop-related crime. It was run by John Davison and, as we had worked well together before, I was pleased when he asked me to join his team of PCs, which included John Adams and Steve Blower among others. Steve was to pay me quite a compliment: an old-school PC he announced one day that I was probably one of the best WPCs with whom he had ever worked. This was a tribute coming from him, but we did make a good team and managed to have a good time too. That's always a bonus. Our zone of operations was Wood Green Shopping City and the surrounding streets. We were walkers, not attached to a team. This meant I was no longer part of Team 5. We were a specialist independent group that operated out of Wood Green station and dealt with any shop-related crime, such as shoplifting and theft, street robbery, lost children, disputes in the shops and parking tickets.

If you ever want to get into a fight, then issuing a parking ticket is the way to do it. It comes with a cast-iron, copper-bottomed guarantee. One man, a Greek-Cypriot, took exception to me giving him a ticket. His behaviour ranged from objectionable to verging on loopy. Ultimately he went so far over the top that I arrested him for a breach of the peace. Overall, though, I enjoyed my time on the Shop Squad. I was part of it for the six months before I left to join the ARVs in July 1994. Although I missed some of the excitement of driving, as well as the calls that required a faster response than a walking PC could provide, mostly it suited me. The hours were better, there were no nights and only a few lates, which was much more appropriate for me as a mum. It meant that not only could I spend more time with Ben but also that I had some possibility of a social life.

I was out on the Shop Squad with Marion one day when a man we were watching suddenly broke into a trot and, as he did so, threw a knife into the gutter. As he ran off we chased after him through the covered walkways of the Shopping City. I kept Hornsey posted via a full commentary on the radio, but I was wasting my breath. Hornsey heard none of it, as the PR couldn't get a signal under cover. When we emerged into the fresh air — perhaps 'fresh' is pushing it for Wood Green High Road — we eventually caught up with him. Hornsey had no idea of our whereabouts, but despite this failure of technology to summon help we made a successful arrest. Marion was not amused and told me so in no uncertain terms: 'That's the last time I come out with you. Something always happens when you're around.' Her words were more prophetic than she would have cared to believe.

Although I thought the Shop Squad a good thing, there were one or two aspects of it that I believed could be improved and developed. I felt that a side of crime prevention that is sometimes overlooked is spending time and money on education and training so that the public are better informed on how best to defend themselves against street muggings or shop crime. My plan was to go on the self-defence course, qualify as an instructor and then offer self-defence training as a community resource to local shops and businesses. We would also open it up to the general public and to our own officers.

I did the course at Hendon, and one afternoon I took part in an exercise known as the Blue Man. It was carried out in the 'dojo', a large room at the Training School, the walls and floor of which are padded. It is where police recruits practise their judo and wrestling holds. We were blindfolded with black-out goggles and walked into the dojo knowing that in there someone was poised to attack. The object of the exercise was to rely on all our senses, except sight. The attacker was padded for his own protection, the room was padded and I was blindfolded. I was not able visually to assess him or his tactics. There were other students in the room, so, friend or foe, you had to have your wits about you.

Even now it makes the hairs on the back of my neck stand up just thinking about it. In those days I was wary enough. To me, after the stabbing and everything, it was a totally realistic exercise. With my heart pounding, I adopted a warrior-like pose, then just listened and waited, waited and listened, minutely adjusting my position from time to time, my nerves at full stretch. Presumably because the exercise was no pretence to me, I was really very good at it. After what felt like a lifetime, but was in reality only ten or fifteen minutes, I wanted an end to it. So I let him get me. When I took off my goggles and returned to the real world it was much more than a huge relief. Afterwards, during debrief, several of the participants were distraught. For them, like me, it had brought back past traumas: one woman was reminded of when she was raped.

A few weeks later John Davison was having a drink and a chat with the PT instructor, who had acted as our assailant that afternoon. He was fulsome in his praise of me when John mentioned my name and he realised that we were colleagues: 'She was fantastic — the best on the course and way above the rest.' I found this hilarious, because I knew exactly why: if I had been good, it was because I hadn't been able to fake it. My fear was real, and there's nothing like terror to keep you on your toes.

By now I knew how to administer a forearm smash and a crippling knee in the groin, amongst many other simple but highly effective techniques of self-defence. I'd enjoyed the course, it was excellent, and there were two of us at Wood Green station now who were qualified teachers. This all added up to a proper public service. But I was never to put it to much use. We didn't really get the initiative off the ground, despite our good intentions. The best-laid plans sometimes come to naught. I regret to say, I was distracted. I had other ideas in mind.

CHAPTER 9

ONCE IS AN ACCIDENT, TWICE IS UNLUCKY, THREE TIMES ...

MY THIRD BRUSH WITH DEATH

I'd become a shot on the ARVs in June 1994. It was now early autumn and I was out on patrol, driving one of the Rover 827s on a dual-carriageway somewhere in London when a call came in about tracking a vehicle from an armed robbery. The pursuit required armed assistance. It was the early-evening rush hour, and I set off at full speed, two tones going, lights flashing, other cars moving swiftly out of my way. We were getting a commentary on the main set from Scotland Yard about the position of the vehicle we were after. I didn't have a clue where we were going. Although we were based at Old Street, our patch was the entire Metropolitan area, so I frequently found myself lost. Fortunately my operator, the PC in the front passenger seat, was a bit more clued-up and knew his way around. I was just concentrating on driving and had no idea how much further we had to go when unexpectedly we came across the vehicle we were after at a set of traffic lights. When we thought it was going to turn off up a side-road, rightly or wrongly, we were forced to do a stop on it there and then.

We jumped out of the car, and what followed was almost surreal. There I was, at the peak of the rush-hour and in full public view, standing, weapons drawn, in the middle of one of the busiest highways in London. The traffic was at a standstill around us. All eyes were on us, and through them I saw myself pointing my gun at the passengers in the car and ordering them to get out. All of a sudden I thought, I can't believe I'm doing this. It was really odd to have this all going through my head as I stood there under the full gaze of the rush-hour commuters, with all those people watching me as I pointed a gun at someone. It was a very public performance, and I wasn't too sure about it.

It was exactly a year since that old stubborn determination for which I am infamous had kicked in again, and I had begun to set the wheels in motion to join the ARVs. When I got a place in June 1994 only three women had trodden that path before me. I had considered it then, but Pat wouldn't have it. He felt it wasn't a suitable job for a woman with a young baby. I had just got married and become a mum, and I guess he was right. Obviously he couldn't have stopped me if I had set my heart on it, but for the sake of harmony, or maybe because I just didn't want it enough, I shelved the idea.

I met the same sort of resistance from Barry when I first mooted it to him. He didn't want me to go anywhere near it. He told me in no uncertain terms that I should be training to care for people, not to kill them, that firearms work went against my true nature. He knew me well, in some ways better than I knew myself, but I was too close to it all to see myself clearly, which is often the way. Maybe I should have listened. I chose not to. Oddly enough, although Pat has now left the police service, both he and Barry were in SO19. In fact, Barry still is. But, then, for a while so was I.

Back in the sixties the Home Office's D6 Branch had dealt with civil defence and communications, and within it a Firearms Unit was commissioned especially to train the police in the use of firearms. This had been instigated by the horrific murder in cold blood of three police officers. They were shot dead on 12 August 1966 when they approached three men in a parked car near Wormwood Scrubs prison. TDC David Wombwell and DS Christopher Head were shot with an Enfield revolver fired by one Harry Roberts, PC Geoffrey Fox with a Colt .380 pistol fired by John Dudley. Both Roberts and Dudley already had criminal records. The following day, 13 August, the *Daily Mail* ran a piece on the question of arming the police: 'Is It Time To Give The Policeman A Gun?' Either that or make the murder of a police officer a hanging offence, the secretary of the Police Federation suggested. The hunt for the murderers turned into farce at times, with police not properly trained in firearms having to handle a gun for the first time. It was the Met's biggest armed operation since the siege of Sydney Street in 1911. It became painfully clear that only officers properly trained in firearms should be authorised to use them and also that the number of shots in the police force should be greatly increased.

Ten firearms instructors were attached to D6 to handle all police firearms training. The first men who signed up for the residential course at the Small Arms Wing of the School of Infantry in Hythe in January 1967 were drawn from the RAF, Royal Marines, Parachute Regiment, Brigade of Guards and the Royal West African Frontier Force. From April 1967 the Firearms Unit became responsible for all the Met's firearms courses. Though the Met has always resisted the notion that their firearms wing is in any way paramilitary, it was a job, it seemed, for ex-servicemen. And this, I suspect, was the expectation of those applying to recruit. If I got a place on the ARVs I'd be moving into an area of police work that was still very much a man's world. How much so I would never know until I got there.

I'd taken a fitness test in late December, and I'd already been notified that I'd been awarded the highest mark ever given to a woman. There were practical and written assessments, too, before I received a date in January 1994 to attend the ARV selection board. I travelled up for it on the tube, casually dressed in jeans and carrying my uniform folded neatly in a holdall. I changed in the toilets at the SO19 base in Old Street beforehand and looked particularly neat and efficient because Ben's au pair had put my hair tidily in a French pleat. The assessment for duty in SO19 is one of the most rigorous procedures in the entire force, and the questions they asked me that day were tough and wide ranging. It is right that it was so, because that was only the beginning. Once I was a member of SO19 I would carry a gun and had the power to kill. They had to be sure I was up to the responsibility that went with this.

After the ARV board, which I found as harrowing as these formal assessments often are, I changed back into my jeans and went home. There wasn't any more I could do now but wait. I continued to work on the Shop Squad and to train every day in the gym. I spent all the rest of my time with Ben, and on the rare occasion that I had an evening to myself I went out with a friend to the movies or, even more rarely, on a date. I'd met someone at the ARV assessment day I'd attended at Lippitts Hill, but after a drink and an outing to the theatre, I decided not to see him again. He was perfectly pleasant and a nice person, but I had still not got over Barry, and my enthusiasm for other men was limited.

A lot of half-hearted attempts at romance followed. In the ARVs I got lots of offers. Maybe it was scarcity value, because of the dearth of women, or maybe some men find a woman who works with guns intriguing. I don't mean to undervalue myself, because I have had my share of male admirers, but something changed when I joined SO19. My appeal seemed to rise by several notches. At one stage I was pursued by as many as half a dozen men at once. Rather than feeling flattered by this, I just saw it as extra pressure. A couple of the men who asked me out were married, and I wasn't interested. It was typical of my experience of SO19, especially the Specialist Firearms Officers (SFOs), a lot of them saw it almost as the done thing to cheat on their wives or partners. I felt offended when I'd try to be friends, and they wanted to go a step further. In any case it was to be a long time before I found anyone who matched up to what I'd left behind.

When I phoned for the results of the ARV selection board a week or so later I was put through to Chief Inspector Norman Mackenzie. After the preliminary greetings I was shocked when he told me that I had come top of all the interviewees for the next intake. I was most surprised that I had beaten all those men, because there were some tough characters on board. Later that month Ben went to stay with my parents for a fortnight while I went on a two-week basic firearms course where I learnt to fire the Heckler & Koch MP5 carbine, a machine-gun lookalike, and the Model 10 revolver or handgun.

The MP5 is a robust, German-made weapon that is accurate at a distance of up to 100 metres. Once I was a working ARV officer I was to carry it in an over-the-shoulder body harness. It weighs about six pounds and is just over two feet long. It's not that heavy, but it is unwieldy. Easier to handle is the Model 10, a .38 Smith & Wesson revolver that is nine inches long with a four-inch barrel and weighs only 34 ounces. The .38 bullets had been introduced in 1985 as a result of a building-society hold-up, in which a police bullet went straight through an armed robber, leaving him relatively unharmed, fit enough to continue to point his loaded gun. Both weapons were standard issue for specialist firearms officers on the ARVs. Later, the Glock replaced the Model 10. This self-loading pistol, the SLP, as it's sometimes known, was a joint design initiative between its manufacturers, the army and police agencies. I had to get my head round that too subsequently. Which was just as well: this was the gun I was to aim at Alan McMinn on Boxing Day 1994 and never fired. This is usually the way of it, and the most recent statistics prove it: in 1997 of the 1,765 operational deployments, SO19 officers fired shots only once.

The ten days of training, a mix of fieldcraft and classroom study, took place at Lippitts Hill training camp, an ex-army base just slightly north of Epping Forest. On arrival I was kitted out with a blue boiler-suit, a belt, holster, ear-muffs, glasses and body armour. I was there to learn everything there was to know about those two weapons and how to use them lawfully to stop, not kill, a suspect. Unlike the army, we weren't trained to kill, wound or aim for a specific mark. Our goal was to shoot at the torso, the largest exposed part of the body and its central mass.

I also learnt the basic principles of armed-police tactics. Tactics were vital. If you were armed but didn't know how to behave tactically then it was all, at best, a waste of time, at worst, a waste of life. How to use cover, RV (rendezvous) points and your common sense during an armed operation may seem obvious, but it can go horribly wrong. In Leicestershire some years earlier three people had died because the armed-response operation was insufficiently tactical. Three PCs had gone to a call to find a woman lying dead in the road from shotgun injuries. The gunman had taken refuge inside the house. Two of the officers made their way to the rear of the building to force an entry. A second police car arrived, and two more officers raced up the front drive. They were shot for their trouble, one of them fatally. An ambulance arrived, and the crew, police and neighbours used its door as cover. This was blown when the gunman fired his shotgun through it and killed one of the ambulance men. The third of the first three officers at the scene attempted to radio control but was shot in the head through the windscreen. Eventually the gunman was overpowered as he tried to escape this scene of carnage, but not before he had set fire to the house. This was a wonderful example of how not to do things.

One of the hardest tests of my memory was to learn the names for all the different parts of the guns, from the front sights to the stock pin, the barrel lug to the bolt plunger, as well as the drill on how to load and unload them plus field stripping and cleaning. Then I had to go out on the range to learn how to shoot. I was taught about aiming techniques, positional, close and long-range shooting, as well as range safety and commands and shoot–don't shoot scenarios, all of which was supported by slides and films, including footage from a *Monty Python* episode, which was quite a laugh. The culmination of the two weeks was the classification shoot, in which it was necessary to score an overall minimum hit rate of 70 per cent. This I did.

A lot of it was indoctrination, because that's what you need when you first start to handle a gun. There are fundamental rules, like those for speaking a language or being able to walk or swim, that you simply have to obey, otherwise things fall apart. You don't communicate, you fall over or you drown. With a gun if you ignore the rules you might accidentally kill yourself or someone else. The five-point gun etiquette we learnt parrot fashion mostly begins with the words always and never, and they were drummed into us from day one. Always establish whether a weapon is loaded or unloaded whenever you pick it up, hand it to or take it from any person. Never draw a weapon from the holster or place a selector lever to fire unless you can justify doing so. Make safe any loaded weapon not required for immediate use. Always point the weapon in a safe direction and never at any person unless you can justify doing so. Keep the trigger finger outside the trigger guard unless you believe there is an imminent threat to life. The aim of authorised firearms officers (AFOs) like myself was to prevent loss of life, to protect people not to kill them. Even so, I'd finally found myself at the sharp end.

In the spring there was more: a two-week residential course, at Lippitts Hill again, for the step-up course from the January basic. All the normal shots on the division did the initial course, officers who worked as armed guards at hospitals or patrolled Heathrow airport, but the course in which I took part that April made me into an ARV officer. There were one or two surprises. In *Bonnie and Clyde* and endless car-chase movies, I'd seen speeding cars with their tyres shot out by a round fired from a handgun. But the likelihood of this happening in reality is remote: a normally inflated tyre on a stationary vehicle will stop a bullet from most handguns. Once the wheel is in motion, it's even harder to penetrate it, and even more so as it gathers speed. The effect of the bullet striking the tyre is the same as one hitting a flat surface at an angle and being deflected. The faster the wheel revolves, the more acute the angle becomes, with even less chance of puncturing the tyre. So that was another Hollywood myth deflated.

I found Searching for Armed Suspects in Buildings one of the hardest drills to master. It's among the most dangerous operations that exist on SO19. *Starsky and Hutch* may be most people's idea of how it's done, but preferably it's a job done in threes. And it's much slower and more methodical than it is on TV. There's no encouragement to burst in like you see in *NYPD*. Teamwork is vital with firearms duties. I never worked on my own, and there was a minimum of two to a car. But teamwork I can cope with, scaling a high building fully armed and wearing combat gear, I cannot deal with so readily. My fear of heights had not improved over the years. Some things you never get used to.

Dot was the only other woman in training with me, and in a bizarre coincidence we discovered that we shared the same birthday, 1 May, although Dot is a year younger than me. She is Scottish, and I liked her very much. We still send each other Christmas cards, and the last I heard of her was that she was off sick with a knee injury sustained in training. That April we lived in one of a row of prefabs, where Dot and I had a dormitory to ourselves.

Much like the basic course, this one was intensive but even more so. There was lots of pressure — in fact, the point of some of the training is to assess how well you perform under stress. But some of the pressure Dot and I were under was that as the only two women at the camp we stood out from the crowd. We didn't blend into what was essentially a male environment. I guess we were something of a challenge to the *status quo* and undoubtedly a curiosity. Certainly this is how the younger gunslinger types and their older comrades-in-arms, the crusty old-school-tie brigade, appeared to see us. Traditionally you only ever got into SO19 if you were a Mason. Someone once told me this, and I see no reason to doubt it. Some of the characters I met subsequently were from that cast list. You only have to recall its origins as an outlet for ex-servicemen to know it may well be so.

All eyes were on us. I remember one of the chief inspectors standing at the back of the shooting range watching when we were classifying on the MP5. We had to reclassify on all the weapons we had learnt to fire on the basic course. I was aware of him observing Dot and me in particular. Were we being watched for the right or the wrong reason? Was it about finding fault with us and blaming our gender? Of attributing blame for something that we were not doing right to the fact that we were female? Men's failings are not necessarily put down to their gender. Or were they really trying to establish if we women were up to the task? We were the avant-garde. But was the Firearms Unit of the Metropolitan Police a suitable place for a woman? Were we made of the right stuff, strong enough not only physically but mentally?

As far as the ARV course went, Dot and I were up to the mark, and we both passed. By doing so we were to become only the fourth and fifth female firearms officers, and I was the only mum ever to have belonged to SO19. Although there were a lot of nice, normal men around, it had more than its fair share of macho men, who, I got the feeling, were anti-women. One male instructor who had been there since the age of the dinosaurs dismissed us as a pair of old slappers. Another more enlightened man, Brian Walker, took offence at this and defended us. I wasn't witness to it — something had been said at the final-night booze-up at Lippitts Hill, when the beer started talking — but I heard about it later.

All in all I'd found it tough going. My head wasn't able to process the stress quite as well as it had pre-stabbing. I had to work triply hard to maintain the same level. During the weekend off I felt like curling up in a ball and staying like that. I just lay in bed crying my eyes out. Barry came round to fish me out. I was really struggling. I honestly felt that, like a sponge, I had absorbed as much as I could, and that it was going to be a battle to keep myself buoyant during the final week. Barry drove me down to my parents to see Ben on the Saturday, because I was missing him so much. We all spent the day together, then Barry drove me back that evening.

The second week was more of the same. We had a final assessment in which we had to negotiate a major assault course at the Royal Small Arms Factory, a disused munitions site in Enfield. It was an exercise in open countryside dotted with a scattering of large buildings, up which you had to climb fully armed. There were also targets to shoot as you went. It was full of nasty surprises. You'd turn a corner, and there'd be a target with a gun to greet you. It is one of the hardest courses run by the Met, and some say it ranks with aspects of SAS training. In the end I was just glad to pass, because quite a few people didn't. On the Thursday night of the second week we all got called into the main office one by one and told our result. There was a basic pass percentage of 70 per cent, and I got 78 per cent, a mark that was higher than several of the men scored.

On the Friday we celebrated with a few drinks in the Owl, the pub across the road from Lippitts Hill where I'd been on my first date with Pat. I thought I was about to join a really professional outfit, but that night was a bit of an eye-opener. I'm not saying that all the instructors were the same, but a few of them started to compare notes on one of the women behind the bar about who had and who hadn't slept with her. I couldn't believe my ears, and I'm sorry to say that she was gruesome. What some men will do. It was disappointing. But I soon forgot about it because we all got drunk. It had been a stressful fortnight, and getting out of it was a big release. Eventually the bar games started, the silly boys' games, one of which involved two bar-stools. What you had to do was to lie with your feet on one, your head on another, your body stretched in between. Then you took a third bar-stool and passed it underneath and over you. It was largely a matter of how long you could hold your body horizontal and circle the stool up and over you.

As I watched the men all doing this, I thought, Huh, I can do that. So I did. There I was playing this daft macho game for all I was worth. I kept on and on, and I beat them all. I kept going for ages, because I was so determined to win. There was no support for my back except my stomach muscles, but however strong they were, and they were stronger than most, I had a bad back for weeks afterwards.

During the second week we had attended a talk given by Brian Walker. He was a lovely man, for whom I have a place in my heart to this day. He was so straight with me, so far removed from the gunslingers and crusty old pikes. He had been involved in a shooting a couple of years earlier in which he had been forced to shoot an armed suspect on a stairwell. He told us how having to shoot this person, who had subsequently died, had affected him deeply, not only his sleep but also his mental health. I clearly remember him saying, 'Here you are, all sitting comfortably in a classroom, but I can assure you that something will happen eventually to most of you. One or more of you will have to shoot someone or be shot by someone in the next couple of years.' Well, in my case it was to be sooner than that.

On the Friday I went home, via Childswickham, where I collected Ben. It was lovely to see him. He was always such a good little boy. I can't say that enough. He's a brilliant kid, in spite of everything that has happened in his short life, all the upheavals he's been through. I was constantly in tears at home. You think kids don't see you're upset, and you try not to let them, or you imagine that they are too young to notice. But I'll never forget Ben saying to me a year or two later, after the shooting when we were back in Worcestershire, staying with my parents, 'Mummy, you don't cry so much now. Why's that?' It pulled me up short and made me think, Gosh, he's taken it all in. The tears had begun after the trauma of the stabbing, which had set off the PTSD. But I'd thrown myself so much into my work and studying that I didn't have time to deal with it. And when I started working on the ARVs in the summer of 1994, I was far too busy to give it much thought.

I stayed on the team at Hornsey until May, saying goodbye to all my colleagues on the division at my leaving drink at the Cock and Dragon in Cockfosters. Bob Robinson, the sergeant in charge of Team 5 at Wood Green, was wonderfully generous and paid for all the food that night out of his own pocket. They'd organised a whip-round at the station, and I was overwhelmed by the leaving presents: a microwave, a carriage clock and a barbecue. There were even some gift tokens from Toys R Us for Ben. We had a big booze-up, with lots to drink and eat, and I felt quite emotional. After all, I'd been on Hornsey Division since 1986, and eight years in one job is a big commitment. It'd been my first job, too, and I'd learnt a lot in that time and made some good friends along the way. I didn't dwell on any of this for long, though, because I'm not the sentimental type, and I was looking forward to the fresh challenge of a new start. I'm quite good at moving on. In June, with the weekend as a breathing space, I joined the ARVs.

I was expecting the base for SO19 at Old Street near the City of London to be a really slick and professional centre of operations. After all, it was the north London headquarters of the Firearms Unit, a high-profile specialist wing of the Metropolitan Police. I was disappointed. Where I found myself working was an ancient, rundown Victorian building situated next door to Old Street magistrates' court. Access to it was through a door set into one side of a pair of imposing wrought-iron gates. We all had a key to this, and you'd imagine it was one of those clunky metal jailer's keys that hang on a ring on a chain, just like you see in old movies set on Alcatraz or Robben Island. That set the tone. There was no modern, smart-card entry for us. This was reflected in the Dickensian look and feel of the place, in no way diminished by the gloomily Gothic area in which it was set. Old Street was not an upbeat part of town, although rumour has it that it is now becoming so. London is changing all the time, and the most unlikely places become fashionable. Back then it was a bit of a wasteland. Each time I parked my car I wondered if I'd ever see it again.

At Hornsey I'd been quite well respected, but at Old Street it was altogether different. It felt like starting again, and I had to learn to fit in. I was assigned to B-Relief. No woman had ever worked on B-Relief before. I was the first, and the one and only. My reception was a bit, 'Oh, my God, there's a woman,' as if they'd spotted some rare species from the heart of the Amazonian rainforest. They started as they meant to go on when they called me Bob after the female character in the Elizabethan episodes of *Blackadder* who passes herself off as a man in order to go to war and fight. 'It's Bob,' they'd say. Or Treacle, as in the tart. Or even Doris, though I'm not sure why. Mainly I was Bob. The nice ones, Colin, Archie and Whiffie, said it affectionately, and then I didn't mind. (Whiffie had earned his alias from a note that he left for his wife one day about something to do with changing his socks. The name stuck like glue from that day on.)

There was one sergeant on our relief whom no one liked, a really obnoxious rugby-playing character, who was hopeless at dealing with people. I got the distinct feeling that he was particularly anti-me. He was the first person I'd ever come across who'd taken against me personally. His *modus operandi* was to make disparaging comments like, 'Life's a bitch, and then you marry one,' which were clearly aimed at me. He was rude to the men as well, and he'd have been the first to rub his hands with pleasure if I were ever to have made a mistake. What's more, he would have attributed it to the fact that I was a woman. I felt he was longing for me to slip up, because he watched me like a hawk for the slightest opportunity to make me look small and put me in what he saw as my place. He was obviously not a very sorted-out, happy person, but knowing that didn't help me. I was new, and I didn't want to rock the boat, so I let most of it go without comment. I felt I had to tread very carefully, and I did. But Steve Collard, a PC on my relief who never minded whose feathers he ruffled, used to stand up for me. He became my friend and took me under his wing. He'd complain to our inspector, a nice man, on my behalf. To be honest, it didn't really change anything, though at least it was aired.

I was worried about upsetting people because I was new. I wasn't a troublemaker by nature, and I liked to get along with everyone. I was also keen to make a good impression and progress smoothly up the career ladder. If you get on the wrong side of the wrong people in any job, your prospects may suffer. In those days if you did that at Old Street you could be almost sure that you would never advance. Progress in the department depended very much on who you knew and who you played golf with. It hadn't been like that at Hornsey. But Old Street was run along different lines.

It was traditionally male, and I'd never worked with so many men with such big egos. A lot of the men on SO19 seemed to feel important just because of the job they were doing. Many had an over-developed external identity, which they wore like body armour, or perhaps more like a clamp on the brain function. It was definitely a macho place with a thriving culture of machismo. That's indisputable. Some of the male officers seemed to forget that at the end of the day they were policemen. It got lost behind the gun-toting façade. Not all of them, of course, suffered from the delusion that they were in the SAS, because many were nice, ordinary, down-to-earth PCs, but there was definitely a culture and an atmosphere I had never experienced before. Nor would I want to again.

At that stage there were only five women in SO19, out of some 250 officers. By the time I left there were seven women in a 255-strong unit, an increase of nearly 1 per cent. We were definitely in the minority! As it was unlikely that we'd work the same shift, I was often the only woman on duty at Old Street. That was fine, but what bothered me was the attitude of some of the men there, though never any of those with whom I worked closely. There was a distinctly anti-female sentiment, to which I found myself subjected. It was a particular attitude that I can't quite put my finger on, but it existed none the less, partly to do with the problem some men have with women and guns. From when we are children, little girls are supposed to play with dolls, and little boys with guns. Men go to war and women take care of the next generation. We may think this is stereotyping, and it is. But it is also reality. Many modern parents buy dolls for their sons, though I am not sure that many encourage their daughters to play with guns.

I wasn't trying to change the world. I'd joined SO19 for a variety of different reasons, one of which was that I'd always been motivated to achieve, driven ever onwards by my desire to make something of myself. It overwhelmed me. I was proud too of how my career had progressed so far and was swept along by the momentum of my achievements. What I was less clear about was that in some ways I was equally overwhelmed by a need simply to prove myself. I went after promotion partly to show the Met that I was capable of carrying on as a police officer: I would show them and the rest of the world how I was still as good if not better than anybody else. And I did so partly to convince myself. The more I came up against obstacles, the more I would fight to overcome them. Especially after the two life-threatening traumas I had faced. Look, I had lived to tell the tale. But by working with guns was I also arming myself against the next assailant with a knife? This time I'd show them. 'Don't mess with me. Look, I have a gun.' I wasn't on the offensive, but I was prepared to defend myself. And now, quite clearly, I could.

People do things for all sorts of reasons, sometimes conscious ones sometimes not. In 1992, in Chelsea, the Met formed a Child Protection Team of twelve officers. Of them, eleven were pensioned off with stress-related illnesses. It turned out that those officers who had volunteered for the squad had themselves been victims of child abuse or child violence, and had possibly joined subconsciously to exorcise their own ghosts. Had I become a firearms officer because if someone pulled a gun on me I could do something about it? If so, I wasn't aware how badly traumatised I had been by what had happened to me the day I had met Rupert West.

Though I was wobbly inside, my tough exterior was what I showed the world. Only Barry knew the real me. He would remind me of how capable I was and that I could make a success of SO19 if that was what I really wanted. But was it? No one on the ARV selection board ever asked me whether Rupert West's attack or the IRA bombings had left their mark on me. And, for my part, I was sure that nothing else could possibly happen to me. I wasn't interested in consequences. Neither my past traumas nor the difficulties of my present life as a single mum would deter me from joining one of the most demanding specialist operations in the police service. I ploughed on regardless.

When I arrived at Old Street I was determined to deal with whatever the job threw at me, and the anti-female attitude was just part of what I was up against. I wasn't exactly breaking the mould, because the world has moved on and social conventions are changing, but much remains the same. There is equality of opportunity, but some men still don't want to share their toys. For the ones who weren't sorted it was almost as if they found it emasculating to have me around. For the old-school types who found me most difficult it was as if I was going against nature. The men who minded most were often those who had been in the department a long time and were out of touch with how the world operated outside Old Street station and SO19. They lived hidden away in a male fug in which time stood still. But, when it came to it, our work on the ARVs was not macho heaven. There was no riding into town like Clint Eastwood in any number of spaghetti westerns. We weren't swishing through saloon-bar doors in a lawless one-horse town to sort out the good guys from the bad guys in a huge bloodbath shootout before riding off into the sunset to a new frontier. Our work was about containment, negotiation and defusing. It was more mundane, subtle and controlled than pulling the trigger. In my view that is the sort of work at which anyone can excel, if they so wish, regardless of their gender. I intended to have a go.

But it was tough: apart from everything else the work was tiring and difficult to combine with being a single mum. The travelling in particular was exhausting. I had a long journey from Enfield to Old Street every day, which took me the best part of an hour. All sorts of little things undermined me. Molehills became mountains, such as the day my car was broken into and an attempt made to steal the radio. It wasn't easy being new and having to learn to fit in, especially after Hornsey where everybody knew me and knew what I'd done, and where I had lots of friends. But, to paraphrase a Chinese proverb, I was determined that though the birds of unhappiness flew over my head I would not let them nest in my hair.

There was no induction period at SO19 as there had been at Hornsey. You just learnt the ropes on the job. And there was another major difference: the guns. When you arrived at the station for the start of your shift your first task was to book out your weapons from the armoury. On each shift there were seven ARVs, customised Rover 827s that were fitted with an armoury and able to transport guns safely, operated usually by a crew of three, occasionally two, uniformed officers. Each car would patrol the area of London to which it had been assigned that day, waiting to accept calls for armed assistance, not just calls about guns but about any weapon, including a knife. Sometimes none came, though those days were rare.

Some of the Firearms Wing, probably the gunslingers, felt that a call-out to a knife was beneath them. I had a particular problem with this because it is based on the underlying assumption that a knife is not as dangerous as a gun. This is incorrect, and it is something that used to annoy me intensely when I worked on the ARVs. A knife will always win within 20 feet, because of the reaction time. I knew to my personal cost how lethal a knife could be, and ARVs had been requested to attend our knife attack in 1991. On that occasion, as I have mentioned, it was my husband Steve's car that accepted the call. He has since told me that an ARV car was nearer to us than they were. It had turned down the call because our assailant only had a knife.

Knives and guns apart, on any ARV you were largely detached from day-to-day contact with the public. This was to become my biggest regret because it was an aspect of my job as a PC that I had enjoyed and was good at. I started off not sure whether this would matter, and before long felt certain that it would. Quite early on I began to wonder if being part of an armed-response unit was something for which I was ideally suited. But such a thought was far from my mind during the early days at Old Street, especially with the adrenaline pumping round my body *en route* to my first armed-response call.

It was a call to a suspicious vehicle parked near one of HM's prisons, and we accepted it, racing there with lights blazing and horn blaring. When we got there it was a case of 'Crisis? What crisis?' and a huge anticlimax, albeit a small relief too, to discover we weren't needed. The drive there at high speed through the streets of London had been quite exciting, especially because, prior to that, I'd been on the Shop Squad at Hornsey, doing a lot of walking. Too much time as a plod had made me yearn for the fast lane, but life is never that simple.

There was plenty else to occupy me in what was to be a

short career in the ARVs, and a few incidents during that six months stick in my mind. The armed robbery of a high-street post office in Penge, south-east London, that June is one of them. The raid had gone pear-shaped when three men were seen trying to break into the rear of the building by the manager, who'd called the police. The men involved had obviously tried to escape, one of them not at all successfully. A search of the scene of the crime had unearthed a handgun. Nevertheless dog-handlers tracked the suspect for over an hour until Pete Doherty and I had deployed our guns and joined them as their Alsatians followed his scent. After walking along a railway line for quite a while the dogs stopped by a patch of particularly dense undergrowth on the embankment. They began barking and sniffing, running round in circles and going a bit mad by the tangle of brambles.

We found a great big chap, bare-chested and crouching in the undergrowth, his flesh scratched to ribbons by the brambles. God knows why he had decided to remove his shirt. I took my MP5 from the shoulder strap, pulled it up and pointed it at him, shouting at the top of my voice for him to come out and keep his hands in the air where I could see them. Looking down the barrel of the MP5 at him I watched as he walked towards me; Pete had him covered too. Once he was out and seen to be unarmed some of the other officers took over from us, handcuffed him and carted him off. There was no sign of a gun, though during the chase and the subsequent surrender we had had to assume and conduct ourselves as if he were still armed. Afterwards, when we got back to base, Pete and I were talking about our morning's work. It makes me laugh now to remember what he said about me to the others on the relief, about how horny it had made him feel to hear me yelling at that man to surrender. I didn't live that down for a while. Nor did he. Not even a Good Work Report sufficed to eclipse it.

I was out on patrol another time with an older PC. He was ex-army and rather gruff, a bit of a rough diamond. We were cruising with no particular place to go and I became aware that he didn't appear relaxed in my company. Suddenly, breaking what can only be described as an uneasy silence, he blurted out what was troubling him: 'Uh, I hope you don't mind me saying this, but I don't really know how to speak to women. I've never really had to work with any before. I don't want to appear rude, but I don't know how to talk to you.' It verged on the surreal, but all I could do was to try and reassure him. I was very nice to him, treating him as gently as I would the alien from Mars he thought I was.

'Look,' I told him, 'I'm just like anybody else, I'm not any different, so don't treat me so. I'm just me.' Having spent eight years on Hornsey Division, where I'd become integrated into a department of mostly like-minded people, this was all a huge shock. What he wasn't used to dealing with was nothing compared to what I had to cope with when faced with people like him who had barely emerged from the Dark Ages.

I had other issues with which to contend, more pressing than Neanderthal Man. On 1 September, as part of the advanced-driving course, I was learning some basic first aid. I'd finally been given a date for the driving course that August at the Met's Driver Training School in Hendon, because I needed to have it under my belt to enable me to drive the faster cars that made up the ARV fleet. We had just reached the part that related to stab wounds. For some reason that escapes me now our instructor backed up what she was saying by pretending to stab one of us with a fake knife. I was so shocked by this that, without warning, I started to cry. I felt a bit daft afterwards because there I was in a classroom at Hendon with all my colleagues around me and all the lights on, but for a moment it had seemed totally realistic.

I guess I was particularly vulnerable to the memories that day. What must have been near to the surface was that I was approaching the third anniversary of the stabbing. That afternoon the immediate consequence was that my driving went totally to pieces, but I managed, as usual, to pull myself together. Enough, that is, to get a Class 1 pass in the final exams the following day, 2 September 1994. I'd come second in the group three years to the very day that I'd been stabbed by Rupert West in Wood Green.

The advanced-driving course had taken four weeks, and I found it excellent, though tough. I knew it would be so I'd arranged for Ben to stay with my parents for the month so that I could give it my all. We had a range of things to learn, from pursuits, what they call chasing a bandit car, through to correct braking, acceleration and overtaking, how to come off at junctions and take bends properly. It was mostly the usual stuff, but in two particulars unusual: the speed at which we did all this was often in excess of the national speed limit, and we had to do a running commentary throughout on everything we did and saw. It was a course in how to drive and chew gum at the same time, which is much harder than it sounds. Some days we would drive out of London, and once we found ourselves near Dovers Hill, a place not far from my parents' in Worcestershire. Subsequently when I was on patrol on the ARVs in London I would occasionally, if we were in the area, call in for five minutes to see Ben and make sure everything was OK at home. On this occasion, too, we got to Dad and Mum's to find he'd gone out for the day with my uncle. We managed to locate my parents, out picking vegetables, and I'll never forget my dad presenting my driving instructor with a box of runner beans.

When the course started we'd been split into practice teams and assigned a car and an instructor. In fact we had several instructors, one of whom, Chris Gilbert, was later to become Prince William's driving instructor. Only the best for me! I was also lucky in that the other two students on my car were a good laugh: Bob Grundy, a colleague from the ARVs, and a delightful inspector from traffic, Trevor Adams. They called me Hell on Wheels, which just about sums it up. We used to rate each other's driving as we went along, giving each other marks out of ten. One day I was going round a bend when a voice from the back seat announced, 'That was a Jesus Christ bend. In fact, that was a double Jesus Christ bend.' Even though it was gruelling, we all got along well, and I enjoyed the camaraderie and had lots of fun. I needed a bit of light relief at that point, with all the teething problems I was experiencing as a new girl at Old Street.

I'd been in the ARVs for only three months, and already I was putting myself through my paces. But there was even a shadow over that. Though I never heard anything directly, a rumour was circulating that I'd only been given a place on the course because I was female, that I'd been accorded special treatment because I was a woman. You really had to let it go or you'd go under. Everyone suffered. No one was spared. There was a guy on my relief who had been in SO19 a bit longer than I had and who took the driving course just after I did. He was given a lot of stick beforehand about having to do better than me. He couldn't be beaten by a woman, they jeered. They took the mickey out of him mercilessly.

There were aspects of ARV work that I wasn't too happy about. Like map-reading in the back seat at ninety miles an hour, attempting at full speed to find our way through one of the many parts of London alien to us. That was my least favourite task. I hated it. The person in the back always had to do the map-reading. You'd turn up at a call feeling sick. It was hardly professional. Colin Dixon, a lovely bloke but really mad, was probably the best driver on our relief. When we were on a shout and he was a passenger, he would just sit there with his eyes shut. I remember watching him when I first started and thinking how strange he was. When I asked him about it, he said he was just too scared of other people's driving to open them. It was fine if he didn't look. He couldn't see what might happen.

I'd been driving most of the night, and I'd just swapped with another advanced driver in our crew when we got a call to aid a chase after an armed suspect. We started to make our way over, me in the back, with Pete Doherty, the operator, in the front passenger seat. Pete knew the area and warned the driver that at the bottom of the hill, down which we were travelling at ninety miles an hour, there was a sharp right-hand bend. If he said it once he said it half a dozen times, but it fell on deaf ears. The driver's speed did not slacken. Pete repeated himself again, his voice rising higher, talking faster as he made his point with increasing urgency. Eventually the driver began to slow down, but it was not soon enough for us to make the bend. In an excellent example of bad driving, we went straight on and into a hedge. Although I make light of it now, it was terrifying. Fortunately, after the car had crashed we climbed out unharmed and only a bit shaken up. Soon, in that brush-it-off spirit at which we excelled, we could see the funny side of it. But it might have been different.

And I wanted things to be very different. Though not quite in that way. In an attempt to break out of the downward spiral into which I felt I was allowing myself to be drawn, I had been thinking of applying for a transfer to West Mercia. It is the constabulary for Hereford and Worcester, and Shropshire, which polices the area around where I grew up. I'd always intended to return there, and now seemed as good a time as any to do so. Life was getting a bit too much. The little incident in the classroom at Hendon when I'd become upset when the first-aid instructor faked a stabbing had made me realise that I was actually more affected by the things that had happened to me than I'd realised. The last November I'd seen a leaflet about PTSD at a talk we'd had at Lippitts Hill, and from symptoms listed in the leaflets distributed at the end of it I could only think, That's me, that's how I feel. I went to pursue this with Occupational Health, and they sent me to see a counsellor. But, as it turned out, that only made me worse. What with the stress I'd suffered after the stabbing and the bombing, the trouble I'd had getting over Barry and now the complications of my new job I just longed for a fresh start. I put in my application for a transfer to West Mercia Constabulary and then just had to wait and see. I soon learnt they had a freeze on recruitment, but they put my name on file. For now I'd have to bide my time and make the best of things on the ARVs, but at least I'd set things moving.

I was more than a little restless, but, as always, what kept me on a relatively even keel were my friends. Marion had been staying with me on and off during 1994 after she'd split up with her boyfriend Andy. We went to Goa together in October that year, leaving Ben behind with my parents. I needed a break, but I missed him. It would have been difficult to take him because of all the vaccinations and injections he would have required. I wasn't happy about him having so many when he was not quite four, and neither was he!

I came back in time to attend the official presentation of the Queen's Commendation for Brave Conduct at New Scotland Yard on 22 November, which had been announced in the *London Gazette* of 1 July. There, in front of Ben, my parents and Barry, among others, Her Majesty's Lord Lieutenant of Greater London, Field Marshal The Lord Bramall, presented me with two silver oak-leaf pins from the Central Chancery of the Orders of Knighthood, St James's Palace, SW1. There was one with a clip and one with a pin, and they could both be worn on the lapel of my uniform, which I wore with pride that day. I also received a certificate signed by John Major, who was 'charged to express Her Majesty's high appreciation of the service rendered'. There were lots of us there to receive various awards for different acts of foolishness. I use this word advisedly, and in no way wish to diminish anyone else. It is how I feel now about some of my own actions over the years.

Prior to the individual presentations and hand-shaking, a short résumé about each of us was read out to explain what we'd done to deserve the honour. This happened at all the presentations and, somewhat chillingly, at an earlier ceremony the George Medal had been posthumously awarded to immigration officer Ng Hung-shek who died in March 1990 while chasing armed robbers in Hong Kong. For others there had been a happier outcome, and the Queen's Gallantry Medal was presented to Alan Clark, an off-duty army private who had rescued two children from a burning house. Also honoured with the Queen's Gallantry Medal were David Moffett of the RUC, Sergeant Peter Wiltshire of the Met and Securicor guard Henry Spencer. Other Queen's Commendations for Brave Conduct honours included Met officers PCs David Nicholls and Edward Deegan, and a London doctor's receptionist Marjorie Condie, for dealing with a mentally disturbed man in possession of an air pistol and a knife. Then there'd been WPC Leslie Harrison. This was an award that really shook me up. In Liverpool eighteen months earlier WPC Harrison had been stabbed through the heart by a burglar. I'd acknowledged her ordeal at the time and sent her a get-well card. But her gallantry award came only a few days after she was forced, at the age of thirty-one, to leave her job as a constable because of her injuries. I'd read about her in the *Police Review* that July, under the headline of 'WPC's Heartbreak At Forced Retirement'. And I'd thought, There but for the grace of God ...

Afterwards there was afternoon tea, and we all had photographs taken. I still have them, some of me with my family and Barry, whom I'd felt it appropriate to invite as he'd seen me through it all, and another of me standing sandwiched between Lord Bramall and Sir Paul Condon. Hornsey Division had organised a bus from the station to take the four of us, plus our respective families, to and from Hornsey and New Scotland Yard, so as soon as the photos had been taken we all climbed back in the bus and headed for home.

It's a great shame, I know, but I didn't really enjoy the day. There was no real understanding or acknowledgement of the experiences we'd endured to merit those honours, and the presence of several high-ranking police officers handing out medals and comments at the presentation ceremony didn't help much either. We were the foot-soldiers. When was the last time they'd got their hands dirty? How much did most of them know about what happened at the grass roots? About how our lives had been turned upside down? I felt that some were basking in the reflected glory of our actions, which to us had been life-threatening and a great misfortune. Whatever it was, I didn't much like the spotlight being on me again.

One of the senior officers, in the usual attempt at small-talk common on such occasions, said something to me along the lines of 'I expect you've got over all this by now, my dear.' I found this another fine example of the lack of empathy I was beginning to expect from those in the higher echelons of the Met. I refused to be patronised and responded with a frankness that perhaps he wasn't expecting, my patience stretched to breaking-point by the fantasy such ceremonies engender: 'With respect, it's not the sort of thing you ever get over, sir.' Your life goes on, but you never forget.

As Christmas 1994 drew nearer I had to face up to the fact that the ARVs weren't really for me. If I was completely honest, I wasn't enjoying the work. Driving round in a car with no contact with the public, primarily to turn up at armed incidents wasn't what I'd joined the police for. I didn't thrive in the predominantly macho environment and atmosphere, nor did I relish dealing with the attitude problems that prevailed at Old Street. I was becoming clearer in my own mind that I might move on. I wasn't doing what I was best at, which is dealing with people, communicating. There's really only one language that a gun speaks, and it doesn't leave much scope for dialogue.

CHAPTER 10

THE HEARTBREAK: ENOUGH IS ENOUGH

On Boxing Day 1994 Alan McMinn pointed his .38 revolver at me and fired. I was lucky. If the trajectory of the bullet had been about half an inch more lateral it would have destroyed the blood vessels and nerves running through the back of my knee with disastrous consequences. I'd joined the police because I wanted to help people, and I'd ended up training to kill them. I was a long way from where I'd started. And I'd nearly died myself.

It was ironic, considering what had happened to me just a week earlier. I was out on a training exercise at Lippitts Hill, tracking an armed suspect — in reality, one of our instructors. In exposed terrain he got the upper hand and started shooting. We returned fire, and I was wounded in the exchange. In the spirit of the occasion I slumped to the ground and was dragged under cover, to have first aid administered. Of course, because it was a training exercise our suspect was shooting blanks. Another of our instructors, Archie Andrews, was overseeing things, and it was he who pronounced that I'd been shot in the leg. Considering what happened only seven days later, his words were uncannily prophetic.

I was taken by emergency ambulance to the Accident and Emergency Department of Chase Farm Hospital in Enfield. I was rushed straight to the resuscitation room where I was seen by the trauma team. My medical notes record that there were entry and exit wounds on the medial aspect of the right knee. The wound was entirely typical of the damage caused by a high-velocity bullet, the exit, or posterior, wound more ragged than the entry wound. But I'd been especially lucky because the bullet had not damaged any bone: the entry and exit wounds were to the side of my kneecap. They operated on my right knee quite quickly under general anaesthetic, giving me antibiotics via a drip. Then they sewed me up. To this day I have two inch-long scars at the back and front of my right knee.

Barry had arrived in Casualty a few minutes after me. A local PC had contacted him while he was relaxing up the road at his mother's house near Chase Farm Hospital. He stood beside me, watching over me like a guardian angel as they worked to save my leg. 'Enough's enough, Helen,' he said. 'You've given enough now.' And I suppose I had. Within three years I'd been stabbed, involved in an IRA bomb explosion and shot, all within a radius of fifty yards. Was someone, somewhere, trying to tell me something?

When he felt able to leave me, Barry went off to phone Marion, who arrived after I'd come round from the anaesthetic. I owed Marion one. She'd been coming over to me for supper on Boxing Day. Instead she had to rustle up something for herself and visit me not at home but in hospital, where, in a reversal of fortune, I had roast dinner the next day, brought to me by Barry's mum, Mary. After the operation, among the first faces I saw as I came to in the recovery room were those of Superintendent Mike Waldren, the officer in overall charge at the Old Street base, and Commander Roy Ramm, the man in charge of all SO departments. Colin Johnson, the police constables' Police Federation rep for SO19 at Lippitts Hill, came along later. CJ, as he is known to his friends and familiars, had tried to persuade senior officers to let those involved in the shooting visit me immediately I'd come round after the operation. He felt it might help their peace of mind to reassure them that I was OK. Apparently they would not allow it.

What couldn't be stopped was the constant stream of friends and family who arrived from then on to offer me their love and support. Even the ambulance driver who'd driven me to the North Mid after I'd been stabbed turned up. My parents arrived with Ben, but not without some planning because I'd borrowed their car. It was parked near the SO19 base at Old Street. I'd taken it to drive back up to London in the early hours of Boxing Day morning. In the end my brother Peter drove them up, and it was reassuring to see them all. Ben was very quiet and kept his own counsel at my bedside. I felt for him, poor little boy.

Just like before, there were bouquets of flowers and piles of cards. But this time I was going to do things differently. There would be no press. There was a police guard at the door to the ward to make sure that no media got to me. I did not want any press coverage. They had got it wrong in the past, so why should they get it right this time? I was fed up with the distortion but most of all with the intrusion on my privacy at a time when I wanted some peace and quiet in which to lick my wounds. I also wanted my desire for privacy and anonymity to be respected. I was not for public display either to gain sympathy for the police service and the terrible job we all had to do or to help newspapers in their circulation wars. I no longer wanted to be treated like a commodity. But I had not reckoned on the tenacity of the press. Somehow my ordeal was leaked to the papers, and it was no surprise that the story that appeared in the *Daily Mail* on 9 January 1995 was full of the usual inaccuracies and economies with the truth.

The headline declared I was 'Shot, Knifed, Bombed —

And Ready for Duty'. It was followed by a piece that reported my apparent determination to return to work as soon as possible. Who'd told them that? I wondered. Not me. I hadn't spoken to the press. It turned out that the whole thing was a construction, lifted from the interview I had given in hospital in September 1991 when recovering from Rupert West's knife attack: 'I've been assaulted before but not to this extent. I didn't have much time to react. It happened too quickly. At first I thought I'd been thumped, but I was a bit frightened when I saw all the blood.' These were remarks I'd made after I'd been stabbed.

Then there were the usual inaccuracies. Apparently I was in hospital recovering from the injuries I had sustained during the shooting. In fact, I'd been out of hospital for nearly two weeks by the time the story was published. I'd been stabbed in the armpit. I had not. I was PC Kelly, wife of a policeman. I had reverted to my maiden name at the time of my divorce in 1993. And so it went on. To make matters worse the story was accompanied by the photo taken of me in hospital with my arm in a sling that had appeared in the press coverage of the stabbing in 1991.

Over the years the *Mail* had made full use of this photo. It had not only appeared in 1991 and again on this occasion in 1995, but also in the version that showed Jeni and me side by side in our hospital beds. That time, in 1992, it was used to illustrate an article on male aggression towards women, written by Mary Kenny that December. Her main thesis was that it wasn't fair to put women in the front line in the battlefield, that sending two women police officers out on patrol together was tantamount to giving brutish men the green light. Of course, this was not the reality of our incident, but she wanted to make a point about something else. It was even more misleading and ironic because of what happened to John Davison.

At some point in the January 1995 article, there was a quote from one of my colleagues, who commented, 'She is a very brave officer indeed. We are very proud of her. She tried to keep quiet about her latest injury.' Well, I certainly had. And I'd failed. But not with everyone. At least the Met respected my wishes, though not without a fight. Commander Roy Ramm, who wrote to me on 30 December to wish me a swift and complete recovery and thank me for all I had done, had phoned me at home in Enfield to find out why I was so against any publicity. I explained, and also told him that McMinn's family lived near me in north London. I was scared by their proximity. It made me feel vulnerable. Although it was unlikely, under the circumstances, I didn't want to encourage any reprisals by letting them know how close I was to them. Ramm assured me that if there was any trouble with McMinn's family they would rehouse me. Oh, no, I thought, that would be the start of something to which there is no end. That wouldn't do at all.

Nor would it do for me to let the *Mail* publish what they wanted about me without any comeback. My request for privacy and anonymity had been conveyed to the media by the Met's press office, but it had been ignored. I was not prepared to turn the other cheek. At the beginning of February I decided to write to the paper's editor, Paul Dacre, to set the record straight. It wouldn't change things, but at least I'd get it off my chest.

A reply came from Lawrence Sear, the *Daily Mail's* managing editor, dated 9 February and sent to me at Old Street, care of Chief Inspector Bernard Beer. Mr Sear was sorry to hear that the *Mail's* coverage of the shooting had caused me further trauma. He wanted to assure me that they had hoped it would be seen as a tribute to my courage and provide positive publicity for the police. The last thing they had wanted was to cause me, my family or friends any further distress and asked me to accept their apologies for this. The paper understood, he went on to write, from senior colleagues of mine, that the story would be good publicity for the Firearms Unit and would highlight the potential dangers its officers face in the line of duty; that the piece coincided with a charity appeal on behalf of injured police officers that featured me in its material but did not name me. Then he dealt with the specific points I'd made about the story's inaccuracies and ended his letter with the hope that I was now well on the road to recovery. Well, I wasn't.

I was out of hospital and home by 28 December. My mum stayed on in Enfield to look after Ben and me for the next two days. The phone never stopped ringing and I had a constant stream of visitors. One of them stands out especially in my mind: the Metropolitan Police Commissioner, Sir Paul Condon. It was a very low-key call, and he arrived one afternoon out of uniform. His driver waited in his car outside for the half-hour he was with us. There was no fuss, only from Ben, who kept saying, 'The Bishop is coming.' He'd got this into his head somehow, and it made Paul Condon laugh when I told him. He talked to us about his daughter and about being a parent, about how unique my situation was. He knew of no other officer who had been through three life-threatening incidents in as many years. He reassured me that I shouldn't worry about the future. Later he wrote me a personal letter that I found very helpful, but which I have now lost.

Mum couldn't be away from Dad and the business for long, and after a couple of days she went back to Worcestershire, taking Ben with her. I didn't want him to go, but I still wasn't fit enough to deal with the demands of an active four-year-old. That New Year I spent with Marion. Against all the odds, we had intended to welcome in 1995, but by the stroke of midnight we were both fast asleep on the sofa in front of the TV. By the middle of the first week in January, despite high doses of antibiotics my knee was getting no better. In fact, it had got worse and was inflamed and swollen.

When I'd left Chase Farm Hospital they had told me I must return for physiotherapy but meanwhile I should exercise and keep fairly mobile. This I'd done by taking light walks. During one of the physiotherapy sessions I noticed my wound was weeping badly, and by the next day it was swollen and stiff. I soldiered on for a bit, but became more and more worried as it got worse. Early in the new year John Benson, a colleague from the SFO, had phoned me at home to wish me well. He had been shot several years earlier so he was especially sympathetic — and informed. During the conversation he had expressed concern that the medical team at Chase Farm had stitched up both the entry and the exit wound. He told me that in his opinion this was not the appropriate treatment because the wound needs to be allowed to drain away any rubbish that gets in with the bullet. Otherwise there is a risk of gangrene. He'd been treated at Woolwich Military Hospital, and he suggested that I should get myself there. They were the experts in this kind of injury, and they'd sort me out. To do this I had to go back to my GP for a letter of referral.

I was considering this option when I attended a debriefing session on 6 January in the Met's Welfare department at Wellington House. I'd requested this for all of the officers who'd been involved with the McMinn shooting. It turned out to be only slightly helpful, but it was better than nothing. While I was there, in an attempt to assuage my immediate anxieties, I managed to see Dr Johnson, the director of Occupational Health who had referred Jeni Lawson to Ticehurst. He was on duty at Wellington House that day, took one look at the wound and without a moment's hesitation referred me immediately back to Chase Farm. I was taken there at once, driven straight from Wellington House to the hospital in an unmarked police car.

At 3 p.m. I was readmitted and late that night underwent a second operation. This time, under anaesthetic, the surgeons fitted a drain to the exit wound. Before I was discharged the following day I asked the staff how I should best take care of the wound at home. Would a district nurse visit me? If not, what exactly were the aftercare instructions? I didn't receive detailed information.

So it went on in a catalogue of woe. Two days later the wound was weeping profusely again, and not improving. By this time I was beginning to feel despondent and angry about my medical care. I was also depressed and needed not to be on my own. Consequently I was still staying with Marion. It was a Sunday, and Jeni Lawson joined us. That afternoon we all decided that enough was enough, and Jeni got the ball rolling by paging Evelyn Hickey in Occupational Health, who had given me her card. It was vital to get my appointment at Woolwich Military Hospital sorted out before my leg got any worse. But when Jeni got through to her, Ms Hickey was sympathetic but couldn't help because it was her weekend off. Unfortunately my knee didn't function according to those time restrictions. In any case, she helped us as much as she was able, which was to suggest that we contact the base at Old Street. This we did.

By now I was desperate for reassurance from someone who was expert in gunshot wounds. I began to worry that I might lose my leg. It got that drastic. Your mind goes round and round in circles. I was trying my best to stay calm, but I felt overwhelmed. I'd had two general anaesthetics within a fortnight and two spells in an operating theatre, hordes of visitors and well-wishers as well as endless phone calls. I didn't want to ask too much of anyone, and I certainly didn't want to go to pieces in front of anyone. The result was that I had to put on a bit of an act, while inside I lurched from emotional numbness to desperation. The worst of it was that Ben was back with me. I love him dearly, but a bright, healthy four-year-old needs a lot of attention, which I found it hard to give him right then.

My case went back and forth in a game of ping-pong between Marion, Jeni and me on one side and the Met, in the shape of Occupational Health and SO19, on the other. The letter of referral from my GP had become a stumbling block. But on Monday the ninth, when Jeni and Marion, Ben and I had returned to my flat, an active SO19 unit collected it and took it directly to Woolwich. By the eleventh we'd heard nothing, but a district nurse arrived to dress and clean my wound. Unfortunately, the drain came out, and so she packed the wound, effectively closing it again, and then she left, reassuring me that someone else would be along in the morning to dress and clean it. Overnight my knee became very tender and sore, turning red and inflamed, this time accompanied by a burning sensation. I was in so much discomfort that the following day, the twelfth, I went back to Chase Farm, where it took them an hour and a half to remove the packing, a process that, to say the least, was excruciatingly painful.

When I got back to my flat in Enfield and relayed the morning's activity to Jeni she immediately telephoned Superintendent Waldren at Old Street. She insisted that I should be taken to Woolwich at once. He told her he would look into it. He must have pulled some strings, because on the thirteenth a marked, operational ARV arrived to take me from my flat in Enfield to the military hospital in Woolwich, south-east London. We drove there over the Thames via the Woolwich Ferry, three male officers, whom I knew only slightly, and me. The driver, who came into the hospital with me when we got to Woolwich, was quite pleasant, but the officer who sat next to me was a bit starchy. At Woolwich I was seen by Brigadier Brook-Stein. He was very clear that I was to attend there daily as an outpatient for the wound to be cleaned, dressed and assessed. I was not, on any account, to do any physical exercise or anything active at all, including physiotherapy. I had to rest completely. With these instructions I was allowed home.

On the way out of the hospital building, a call came through on the driver's PR that his ARV crew had agreed to go to a call to an armed robbery in Palmers Green. This is a backwater suburb of north London, famous mostly for the poet Stevie Smith and its relative tranquillity. Something had stirred things up, and it was going to take us a lot longer than the average response time of 9.8 minutes to get there. It couldn't have been further away from where we were, though it wasn't far from my flat in Enfield, to which I was about to return. The driver didn't appear too happy at this news. He seemed sensitive enough to be aware that chasing across London to an armed-response call might not be the thing to do with me in the car. While I was with them they were operating as an ambulance of sorts. But the call had been accepted, so we went, mile after mile with sirens and lights flashing; I was rushed back to north London sickeningly fast. We got there in half the time it had taken to arrive from there to Woolwich, but it was not soon enough. It was all over by the time we arrived.

As I'd left Outpatients at Woolwich I had begun to relax and feel confident, for the first time since I'd been shot two-and-a-half weeks earlier, that I was getting excellent treatment. I could start to think of other things. But my sense of relief was short-lived. *En route* to north London my mind raced with the unfairness of it all. Here I was, an officer off sick through gunshot wounds, being driven at eighty miles an hour through the streets of London to a shootout. In my opinion it was more than unfair; it was inhuman. Sadly, it was what I had come to expect from the Met. In my view it is a very good example of how it operates and of its dysfunctional approach to officers hurt in the line of duty, who are never given the dignity of being treated as a victim of crime.

I went home feeling about two inches high. I had not been able to say a thing about it in the car. Not one expression of outrage. I was too traumatised and upset for the words to come out in the right, or even the wrong, order. I'd been the victim of a violent crime. Was I now expected to shrug it off and get on with my life as if it had never happened? Not only that but I'd also had to fight to get the best treatment for my gunshot injury, when I worked for an outfit that was a specialist firearms operation. Why was there no system in place within SO19 to deal effectively and compassionately with its officers when they were shot in the course of duty?

When I got home I crawled on to the sofa and lay there for what felt like hours. The phone rang. I answered it, thinking it might be Jeni. She'd been looking after Ben for the day and, no doubt, was ready to bring him back home. Instead, it was someone from the base at Old Street, a colleague. He had phoned to tell me that McMinn had been talking. He'd been blabbing on about what had happened the day he shot me. He said that he had seen me earlier on in the day, probably when I was casing his flat with Nick Tinning, and he had deliberately picked me out as his target. That made it kind of personal. And that cheered me no end. It felt like the final straw.

For the sake of my four-year-old son and, I guess, ultimately for myself, my sanity and my survival, all I could do was to pick up where I'd left off. It would do no one any good for me to go belly up now. SO19 had obviously got wind of my nightmare outing to Woolwich because the following day, and thereafter for the next ten days, I was driven to the hospital in an unmarked car. But although physically I started to recover, I felt depressed and dispirited. Jeni was in daily contact with me, and one day announced that she thought I was suffering from PTSD. It was no expert diagnosis, but Jeni had been down that road herself and had been treated for the condition. She was pretty sure she was right. I'd finished my sessions with the therapist I'd been seeing just prior to the shooting, because she had decided that I didn't need to see her, but I had been encouraged back in the light of what had happened to me.

I had been allocated the counsellor by Occupational Health, but, as helpful as she tried to be, I found it hard to open up to her and drop my guard, because I didn't feel comfortable enough with her to do so. I still felt we weren't getting anywhere. She knew all this because I told her. I was becoming increasingly down. My asthma was worse, I wasn't sleeping, and when I did I had dreadful nightmares. I'd started to have panic attacks and migraines. If that wasn't enough my periods had stopped, I had chronic irritable bowel syndrome and problems with my hearing. I was operating on a fuse that was getting shorter by the day. I was in a state of hyper-vigilance and found it hard to concentrate. I avoided the news and newspapers like the plague, as well as other people. I was extremely antisocial and more concerned than ever about Ben, about how he was going to fare in the future, about how all this might affect him long-term. My GP had signed me off as suffering from PTSD, but I felt no one appeared to be interested in that.

I'd got the all-clear from the doctors at Woolwich

during the last week in January. After that, I felt I was being ignored. It took a phone call from Barry to galvanise the Met into action, and an appointment was made for me to attend a formal assessment by the Department of Occupational Health (DOH). I was to see Dr David Wallington on 19 April.

I travelled up from Worcestershire for the meeting. I'd moved there in early April to live with my parents because I wasn't managing well on my own. I was becoming increasingly downhearted. Every day I would wake up and worry about when I'd be well enough to return to work. I faced that decision each morning over my first cup of tea. I was too terrified even to contemplate going back and felt like throwing up what little breakfast I could eat. On the day of my appointment with Wallington it was no different. I left Worcestershire early in the morning, and Jeni met me off the train. She was coming with me to support me during the meeting.

We were with Dr Wallington for quite some time, but I felt that it didn't go well, and I left the DOH even more despondent than when I arrived. At times I had been ready to run out of Dr Wallington's room screaming with frustration that I wasn't making myself heard, but fortunately Jeni helped me to keep a lid on things. I was determined to get the help I thought I now deserved. Quite early on in our meeting Dr Wallington had asked me the quite harmless question, 'When are we going to get you back to work?' While I appreciated his reasons for asking me this, it was not at that point my main focus. I was more concerned with the treatment that would best assist my recovery and make me fit enough to return to full duties. He understood this too, but what he could not know was that this was all something that I had lived with for months. So how could I expect him to appreciate my frustration over what had happened during our discussions that afternoon, or, rather, what I felt had not happened. I knew he couldn't wave a magic wand, but I had hoped he would have been able to do more for me. One step at a time, he'd counselled. Did I really want to run before I could walk? I wondered.

When I'd finished I felt exhausted. But I'd only touched on it all. There was still the list of my symtoms that Jeni and I had compiled on the tube on the way there. I still have it, written in a strong turquoise ink. But I couldn't face talking about some of these things, in the circumstances.

We left the building in a state of shock, not able to believe what had just happened to us in there. I felt as if I'd been slapped in the face. If I were a less strong person I'd have been under a train within the hour. But I felt I shouldn't have had to be that strong. Was this really how the DOH treated officers who had been through hell? I felt, rightly or wrongly, I had been given no support or hope.

I felt explosively angry as we walked away from Wellington House. I was beside myself. I'd just met a brick wall while travelling at 100 m.p.h. I didn't know what to do next. I was feeling let down by my employers. I had given them my all, and now that I wanted something back I felt that the door had closed.

En route, the concrete and glass tower block of New Scotland Yard, since 1967 the headquarters of the Metropolitan Police, suddenly loomed before us. 'What,' I reflected aloud, 'would the commissioner say if he knew how we'd just been treated.' He had been very straight with me back in January and told me not to worry about the future, that if there was anything I ever needed then I had only to ask. Jeni didn't miss a beat, and within moments we were standing inside the foyer, requesting an audience with Sir Paul Condon. Jeni was quite clear why we were there: the commissioner had made me an offer, and now we wanted to take him up on it.

It was the day that PC Walters had been shot dead outside a house in Ilford, when he'd attended a call that had appeared on his PR to be a routine domestic. Understandably the commissioner was preoccupied and unavailable. The best they could do for us was to show us into an anteroom, where Jeni was able to speak by internal telephone to a woman called Daphne, whom she understood to be the commissioner's personal secretary. Daphne assured Jeni that she would pass on details of our complaint to the commissioner's staff officer, Matt Baggott. Looking back on this, and remembering how we marched so boldly into the Met's headquarters at NSY, makes me smile, but at the time I couldn't see the funny side of it at all.

We didn't hang about there any longer than we had to because I had a second appointment to keep that day, this one with my counsellor. Jeni was coming too. I had mentioned this to the therapist the last time I'd seen her, so she was expecting me to bring a friend. The hour-long session proved quite useful. She agreed that she would write a referral letter for me to see a psychiatrist she knew at Guy's, someone she valued and had used in the past. This person specialised in trauma. If I preferred, though, she'd refer me to Gordon Turnbull. She left me to think about it for a couple of weeks and let her have my decision at my next appointment, which we made for 1 May. This was my birthday. It wasn't how I would have planned to spend the day in an ideal world, but my world was far from that, so it seemed somehow appropriate.

That session came and went, but I found it less than helpful, and it got me no further with my request to be referred to Gordon Turnbull. Jeni had come with me again, and on our way back to her house, where I was to spend the night before my return to Worcestershire, I once more expressed by reservations about the counsellor to Jeni. I felt that with her I was papering over the cracks.

Back at Jeni's I felt totally exhausted, and it took me a long time to relax. I was depressed. Who wouldn't be after all that had happened over the past few months? Anyone would have felt the same under the circumstances. To cap it all, in the language of understatement that I'd learnt to speak so well over the years, I had just had what I felt to be a less than productive day. And so, with the only touch of melodrama I had ever allowed myself, I turned to Jeni and said: 'Have I got to do something drastic to make it clear how I'm feeling?' This was really a turning-point for me, the moment at which I became angry and desperate for help.

But when you hit rock bottom, really the only way is up. And so it was that later that afternoon Matt Baggott phoned Jeni and told her I could have whatever treatment I wanted. He would be contacting Personnel over my request to be seen by Gordon Turnbull to be assessed for PTSD treatment at Ticehurst House Hospital.

CHAPTER 11

STARTING OVER

'She hates the fuss and believes she's just doing her job. I'm very proud of her. However, I can't help thinking I would love her to find a job within the police force that is equally satisfying but less dangerous.' This is what my mother had to say to the *Gloucestershire Echo* after my third brush with death, as the paper described the shooting. 'I couldn't believe it had happened again — it came as an awful shock. Thank God she survived,' my mother concluded, her words heartfelt. It was true that, physically, I had come through, but my mental health was a different matter.

I went under my own steam to see Dr Bo Mills at Ticehurst House Hospital, a beautiful white stucco Victorian mansion, set in acres of grounds in the lushness of East Sussex. Jeni kindly drove me there and waited for me while I went in for my assessment. This was extremely thorough and included the use of the Clinician-administered PTSD Scale, an instrument known as CAPS. I answered a variety of questions that ranged from my eating and sleeping habits to the wider ones of my hopes and fears about the past, present and future. Dr Mills diagnosed me as suffering from chronic PTSD. In an interview that had lasted ninety minutes, for much of it I was uncharacter-istically in tears. It was quite simply a huge relief to have it confirmed, to know catagorically that I was ill and not going mad.

I felt that I had at last found a place where people cared and understood, where I believed I would receive the help I needed to get my life and myself back on track. It felt as if I'd finally reached the safe haven of a harbour after a very long time at sea. According to Bo Mills, there was a possibility that I could start my treatment immediately, but such an option was not available to me because the Met would not consent to fund me. Nevertheless Bo Mills agreed to send the bill to Matt Baggott in the commissioner's office, who, in turn, agreed to get it paid. Baggott kindly wished us luck and repeated his earlier promise that I must have everything I needed. In a session with the Hendon psychiatric unit that followed on 18 May he was as good as his word, and I was referred to Ticehurst for treatment. But the wheels turned slowly, and I was appalled and distressed by the unnecessary delay. I'd been given the green light at the beginning of August, but I didn't get to Ticehurst until October. For the months in between I lived in a twilight world haunted by the ghosts of incidents past.

I dealt with this in a variety of ways, one of which was to attempt a little exorcism. This I did one day in the company of Nick Tinning when we drove to the scene of the shooting. It was our way of banishing that particular ghost. And my friends helped as best they could with the rest. They say that you can count your true friends on the fingers of one hand, and I now know how true that is. It was Marion and CJ, Barry and Jeni who got me through and did all they could for me. They were all wonderful. I was cracking up, and they were there for me. At the end of the day, though, everything I received from the Met I had to fight for.

Barry had been there from day one, though he backed off after a while, for both our sakes. To this day we are still friends, and I see him from time to time. His life, like mine, has moved on, and he is now a sergeant in charge of a specialist firearms team, one of the toughest jobs going. Jeni was also a stalwart, and wrote letters and contacted people on my behalf. Marion was her habitually wise and reliable self. She still is the best friend I could ever wish for and is now godmother to Steve's and my daughter, Molly, born after all this was over.

From time to time, in those terrible weeks and months during the spring, summer and early autumn of 1995, I would suddenly feel overwhelmed, and distress would wash over me in waves. How much more could I endure? I just wanted to get into my car and drive away, but I couldn't even do that as I was on my own, and someone had to be there for Ben. Sometimes thinking about the effect of all this on my young son was like driving a stake through my heart. I had no idea how he was really coping. Ben is a bright, sensitive child, who picks up easily on my moods. On a couple of occasions he had asked me who would look after him if Mummy died. If I never hear that question again in my life it won't be long enough.

Fortunately, I had one true ally with the influence I required to help me fight my corner. And that was CJ. Everyone knows him. He's the most fantastic person for whom everything is possible. After he'd visited me in hospital following the shooting, he had remained involved in my case, giving me helpful advice and support. Jeni had written to him at Lippitts Hill, sending him a long letter detailing what seemed to me to be the trail of indifference I'd endured. He became a great friend, especially valued because there was never any hidden male agenda behind all he did for me. His family were equally supportive, and his wife, Terri, and their two daughters always welcomed me into their home, as they still do today. CJ even gave a speech on the day I married Steve, but much earlier, in September 1995, he spoke up for me when he accompanied me to a meeting with the DOH. He came with me to every such appointment I had thereafter. From then on, we were always permitted the courtesy of seeing the CMO in his office rather than at his clinic. It's odd how much more amenable they were when he was around.

CJ also helped me in other, less obvious ways. He was conscious of what I'd been through and wanted to do what he could to enable me to come to terms with it. With this in mind he arranged for me to meet Sandy Kelly, the victim of an IRA attack in which he and a colleague had been shot during a random stop on the A64 in north Yorkshire. First they murdered Special Constable Glen Goodman. Then they turned their guns on Kelly before they drove off, leaving him for dead beside the lifeless body of his fellow officer. Talking to Sandy Kelly was an extraordinarily heartening experience. If he had lived to tell the tale, then so would I. I can only try to express the effect that meeting and talking to him had on me. It was humbling, but mostly it was transforming.

CJ was staunch in his support of me. And that was just as well because no one was going to make it easy. In August the Met informed me that though I'd been on full pay since the December shooting this arrangement was due to be reviewed. My response was a bullish, 'If they think they can cut my pay, just let them try.' But you never could tell what they had up their sleeve, and for all my bluster I was worried stiff.

Other things had happened to make me wonder yet again about the way the Met operated. In May, while I was living in Childswickham, I received a phone call from someone who worked for one of the Met's firms of solicitors. He wanted to discuss with me a civil action in progress against the police, taken by someone who had been arrested in an incident in which I'd been involved. When he'd contacted SO19 and was informed that I was away sick, he had explained that he needed to speak to me and had been given my parents' telephone number. When he phoned I was polite but firm and told him very little. I would co-operate when I was well enough, and until such time I was in no state of mind to help. A while later a letter arrived through the post from the same person. It accompanied a typed transcript of the brief statement I'd given him over the phone. Would I please sign and return it to him forthwith? I returned it all unsigned, reminding him I was on sick leave and not fit to comment.

Time was passing, and I felt I was making little progress. I found myself increasingly under pressure as the date of Alan McMinn's trial grew closer. It did not help my state of mind that I had that to get through. It was held in September, and at the Old Bailey, just like Rupert West's. But this time was different, because I was to give evidence. Had I but known it, it was also significant because it would be the last occasion on which I was ever to wear my police uniform. On the morning of the trial CJ picked me up from my flat in Culloden Road, and we travelled south together to the Central Criminal Court at the Old Bailey. The courthouse itself was built in 1905 on the site of the notorious Newgate Prison. In fact, some of the stonework of its lowest storeys is constructed from its ruins. Across the road the Magpie and Stump served execution breakfasts until 1868, when public hangings outside the prison gates were stopped. That must have been a harrowing experience, though some took pleasure in it. I took none at all in the ordeal that now faced me. I found the thought of coming face to face again with Alan McMinn nerve-racking and distressing, to say the least.

But before that could happen I had to run the gauntlet of the press, who were encamped in the street outside the court. We got through somehow, mostly by ignoring them, and once inside we took our seats to watch the trial unfold before us. When McMinn, described as being of no fixed address, took the stand, his evidence from the witness box was a series of denials: of attempting to murder my colleague PC Nick Tinning and me, of wounding me with intent, of two counts of possessing firearms with intent to endanger life, of causing grievous bodily harm with intent to his girlfriend, and of causing actual bodily harm.

When it was my turn to give evidence I told the judge that though I had recovered well physically from my ordeal, mentally I was still traumatised and awaiting treatment for post-traumatic stress disorder. I described what I knew had happened that day, how McMinn had pulled his gun on me as I moved towards him while trying to draw my own gun from the holster. But it was hard to convey the terror of the moment and how it continued to haunt me. How, though I was only doing my job, I was still a human being for whom this experience would never fade into a distant memory. Sometimes it came back to me as if it were yesterday. I would always bear the scars.

McMinn had his own views on the matter, and he didn't see things my way. His defence was elaborate and hung on his depression, how it had led him to consider suicide. He said he had reached the end of his tether after the final row with his girlfriend that Christmas Eve and decided to end it all. But after he had put the gun in his own mouth he decided — conveniently for him, I might suggest — that he could not go through with it. As he withdrew the gun, it went off, triggered, he said, by my colleagues shooting him first. He told the jury: 'I was not aiming at anyone and had no intention of injuring anyone.'

The defence consisted of a barrister, a junior barrister, a solicitor, a solicitor's clerk and a junior understudy. The prosecution was lean by comparison and comprised a Mr Mitchell, the barrister, and a female member of the Crown Prosecution Service. The case began on a Monday and our barrister had only been instructed the previous Friday. The chambers that had originally been instructed had cried off sick, and Mitchell was brought on as the last-minute substitute. I was involved in the shooting, and I hadn't even met the learned counsel for the prosecution. During the second week of the trial, our CPS representation changed, and the new arrival informed us that he was also covering the case in adjacent Court No. 11 where, if there were any problems, he could be contacted. None of this was ideal.

Nor was the Met over-solicitous in its representation at the trial. We are talking about the attempted murder of two of its PCs, yet the highest rank of police officer in court was detective sergeant. Throughout the two-week trial no senior-ranking officer, apart from a chief inspector from SO19 who attended briefly one morning, was ever present. CJ was there only in his capacity as the Police Federation's representative, and had it not been for him there would have been no support at all for us officers involved. Support for us was lacking on every side. We had all been praised by Sir Paul Condon, but where was his senior representative now?

On Thursday 21 September the case concluded, and the

long and the short of it was that the jury chose to believe McMinn. Apart from his extensive legal back-up, he had put on a good show, even crying in the witness box, sobbing into a proffered Kleenex. I think the jury took pity on him and saw him as the victim of the piece. It is an opinion they might have revised later in the light of the string of previous convictions that were subsequently revealed. There was a particular incident from which he emerged not exactly wreathed in glory when he had abandoned one of his partners in crime as he tumbled from his motorbike during a flight from an armed robbery in which they'd both participated. McMinn just left him lying in the road. Were these the actions of a caring, sharing guy pushed to breaking-point and on the brink of suicide? I think not.

Ultimately McMinn was sentenced to eight years' imprisonment, but not for attempted murder or GBH. Instead he was found guilty of unlawful wounding, ABH, possession of a firearm with intent plus three other firearms-related offences. When the jury returned their verdict, McMinn burst out laughing and punched the air in victory, shouting, 'Yes!' Of course, he was right to do so. He knew, as we all did, that he had got off lightly. But the judge must have got to the bottom of things in his own mind, because eight years is almost the maximum sentence he could have given McMinn for the crimes of which he was convicted.

Afterwards I cried as I hugged Nick Tinning in the police room. The court sergeant gave us a small glass of something alcoholic to help us through, and I was smuggled out of a back entrance to avoid the press encampment at the front. But the media had to be dealt with, though the Met got that wrong too initially because there was no one present at the court of a rank substantive enough to address the press about our trial — even though there was a Detective Sergeant present who was the officer in the case. But they got the story anyway, and it is from the *Daily Express* that I earned the plaudit of 'Britain's Bravest Policewoman'. I doubted that I was because, though I appreciated the compliment and I won't deny my courage, the job sees acts of bravery much like mine almost every single week. Another headline, in smaller type, referred to the 'Anguish Of Gun Siege Police Girl', which, though at twenty-eight I was hardly a girl, was more accurate. I was in great mental anguish.

But something had to go my way some time. And it had on one of the few occasions that I'd rung the base at Old Street. I'd had virtually no contact with any of the senior officers there, and what little there had been had been mostly useless. In fact, I'd rung that day to speak to Pat about Ben. Pat had joined the ARVs a couple of months before me, in the spring of 1994, and I knew that tracking him down at work was easier than finding him at home. But he wasn't there either, so I had a nice long chat with a very friendly PC Dempsey who had answered the phone. I didn't know Steve Dempsey at all well. When I'd first joined SO19 he'd come up to me to introduce himself as one of the ARV officers who'd attended the sawn-off shotgun incident in Hornsey a year or so earlier. Of course I remembered him, and we had a good laugh about the expression on my face when he'd shown me that the shotgun was loaded. We'd passed one another in the corridors at Old Street, and occasionally shared a table at lunch or breakfast in the canteen, but that was it. For the eighteen months since my split with Barry I had had lots of male interest shown in me, but by no one who really caught my eye. So why I agreed to go for a drink with Steve when he asked me during that phone call in July 1995 I don't really know. All I do know is that I am now married to him. And all I can say is that, when you least expect it, a light appears at the end of the tunnel.

It took all of CJ's chivvying and Steve Collard's help to get me to Ticehurst that October. During the months of delay I sat day after day in deep despair at the Met's intransigence. Occupational Health appeared to have insufficient understanding of what police officers go through in the course of their work, of the traumatic nature of the job. It seems to me that the Met will never learn about this because, in my opinion, they never seem to listen to those who have been through experiences like mine. I had never asked for much help, and when I finally needed something big-time it was hardly overwhelming. I loved the job and thought it would love me back. But it didn't.

The hub of the delay was money. Eventually it made the wheels go round, though not before Steve Collard, my stalwart colleague from SO19, who, as luck would have it, lived opposite a chief inspector from the Firearms Unit, had dropped by to see him one Sunday morning to put the pressure on. At Ticehurst House Hospital I took part in the PTSD management programme and lived for two weeks in Lowlands Bungalow in the grounds of the main house. My housemates were three strangers. Jim was a former member of the Garda Síochána. He had been jumped on from behind and seriously injured while on duty in the Republic of Ireland. Jane was a civilian, just an ordinary member of the public. She had been involved in an horrendous and harrowing traffic accident. Stephen was a bomb-disposal expert. He had seen a colleague blown up and killed while clearing mines after the war in Iraq. Although we had all undergone different traumatic episodes we realised that we had all reacted in the same way.

One of the most important things we came to understand during our time at Ticehurst was that we weren't mad. That instead our symptoms were just a normal reaction in normal individuals to exposure to abnormal and traumatic levels of stress. None of the people admitted to the PTSD treatment programme at Ticehurst was suffering from mental illness. When I went there in the autumn of 1995 the programme had been tested over a period of three years and had been the subject of intensive research. This had shown that the group approach they used had distinct advantages over one-to-one treatment. This method had been the subject of a BBC 2 television documentary in March 1993. Although originally developed in a military — Royal Air Force — hospital approximately half of the patients treated were from non-military backgrounds, and both groups responded equally well to treatment.

Jim, Jane and Stephen soon became my friends. We cried a lot during that fortnight, but we laughed a lot too, and we didn't want to leave at the end. We'd bonded as if our lives depended on it. Of course, they did, and it is true to say that the treatment I received at Ticehurst changed my life. To say that the benefits for me of going there were enormous would be an understatement. Afterwards, throughout the year that followed, at six weeks, six months and a year, I had three formal reviews with Gordon

Turnbull, a ruddy-faced Scot with a permanent grin and a great sense of humour. But the biggest consequence for me was the way my time there helped me to make my decision to leave the police force.

I'd been a highly motivated officer. I had given my all to the service, an all that had almost included my life. When I'd wanted something back I had had to beg and sweat for it. Now I had learnt to believe in myself, there was no other way but out. If I'd had this sort of treatment earlier, from the time that Rupert West attacked me in 1991, things might have turned out differently. I might have stayed in the job. Instead it took me until June of the following year to make the break. Derek Driver, who I'd first encountered at Hornsey when he transferred there as a chief inspector, wrote some very kind words about me in support of my decision to take early retirement. He ended his profile of me for the solicitors in charge of my case for compensation for my injuries with these words: 'Without doubt she was a fine asset to the Police Service, and she will be missed. Her like, policing can ill afford to lose.'

I was losing something too. It wasn't just a job I was leaving, it was my career, which I had nurtured and for which I had moved heaven and earth. It was a terrible time, and I was facing what has so far been the hardest decision of my life. In June Barry drove CJ and me to Wellington House in an ARV for the interview with the CMO that would irrevocably change my life. I had been dreading this day for months. All the time I had been off sick I had worried endlessly about what I was going to do. Will I? Won't I? I was torn. One part of me, a big part, wanted to go back. The new inner self I'd got in touch with at Ticehurst was pulling the other way. It was a tug of love and a tug of war. In the end I realised I just couldn't take any more. I opted for self-preservation. I had no choice but to leave the police service. During the meeting at Wellington House, I broke down as I gave the CMO my decision.

After it was over I sobbed uncontrollably with CJ beside me to comfort me and hold my hand. It was more than crying. I was broken-hearted. All the pain in my life had swelled into a river of suffering that broke its banks that day. My PTSD had become so chronic by the time I had received treatment for it that I could not reasonably return to my work as a police officer, which might put me at risk of a major relapse into PTSD, at least, given the inevitably high risk of traumatic stressors.

This was the view expressed by consultant psychiatrist R. S. Mackinnon who had reported on me once before, back in July 1993. His second report for my solicitors was also in connection with my claim for damages for my injuries. He was clear that I had relied on my work and professional advancement as a means of dealing with my symptoms, that my strong personality, as he put it, had enabled me to maintain an appearance of normality during the five years he believed I had been suffering from PTSD.

He listed my symptoms: distressing dreams, distress at any news reports of shootings, bombing and suchlike, distress at the time of the anniversaries of the incidents, a frequent sense of reliving my trauma. Although it was not a symptom of PTSD he also mentioned my increasing feeling of my inability to secure psychological assistance from my employers. He wrote of my use of avoidance tactics and an overall numbness of feeling, of the effort it took to avoid thoughts, feelings or discussions associated with each trauma, of my inability to return to work, or any work-related environment, of my feeling of detachment from others, which made it hard to maintain relationships, of a general reduction and blunting in my emotional range, which affected even my relationship with my son, of the irritability, the impaired concentration, the increased startle response and the hypervigilance, all of which had become increasingly dominant after the shooting. While I still had PTSD symptoms, he believed, I was better able to manage them after my treatment at Ticehurst. Before that I had adapted superficially. At a deeper level he nevertheless diagnosed my PTSD as chronic. It was something that might not be triggered only by traumas at work: 'Even outside the police,' he wrote, 'she cannot be said to be free of such a risk.'

I was medically retired on 24 October 1996. A few weeks earlier I had to go through what I hoped would be one of my last encounters with the Met's senior management. My appointment at Lippitts Hill to dot the Is and cross the Ts was with Chief Inspector Bernie Beer. Fortunately, though, as Steve drove us through the camp gates I'd spotted Brian Walker, my erstwhile instructor. Seeing him reminded me that there had been some decent sorts in SO19.

I knew our meeting was never going to be enjoyable, and I did not expect the red-carpet treatment, but I was hoping for some real warmth. The door to Beer's office in the Bungalow, the base for the admin people and the SOs, remained open from the start, and we were continually interrupted by a stream of people. Eventually Steve took it upon himself to close it. I'd imagined we'd be in and out of there in no time, but it was not to be. I did feel that Beer could have been a bit more sympathetic. The worst, though, was yet to come: the moment when I had to hand over to him my warrant card. It had been part of me for so long, and I knew when I passed it to him across his desk that this marked the end of my police career. This small gesture was a huge step for me. In one tiny movement I'd done what was for me the equivalent of traversing the Grand Canyon in one step. When we'd left his office, I finally allowed the tears to flow. But as Steve drove me through the security barrier and out of the training camp I knew we were going to a better place, where they could hurt me no more.

I nearly didn't make it. On 14 October, ten days before my discharge date, I was driving up from the Cotswolds to see Steve in London. It was a journey I'd been doing regularly, this time with Ben beside me in the passenger seat. I had a lot of things on my mind. Happily, one of them was that I had just found out that I was pregnant. But on a less upbeat note I was preoccupied by my imminent departure from the Met. I felt completely upside down and purposeless, as if my life had no structure. Despite my new relationship, my pregnancy, my wonderful little boy and my supportive family and friends, I was rootless and drifting.

We hadn't gone far on the road to London when I found myself wandering off track. Before I knew it I was on the wrong side of the white line and involved in a head-on collision. The car coming from the opposite direction was a write-off, as was mine. Ben and I and the occupants of the other car were more than lucky to escape with only minor injuries. Today I am left with a phobic anxiety about driving, which one of the psychiatrists I have seen considers can be encompassed within a single diagnosis:

PTSD. The accident that day was entirely my fault: my mind was elsewhere.

My thoughts at that time were here, there and everywhere. I had constant flashbacks to my life as it had unreeled over the previous ten years. I had a head full of memories, some good, some bad. And they didn't stop once I'd taken early retirement. They were refuelled constantly, never more so than in the months that followed. I received my pension details from the Met in a package. On its cover, written in bold letters were the words: Enjoy Your Retirement. This couldn't have been more inappropriate if they'd tried. The enclosed literature tried to explain the complex things you should and shouldn't do. My financial adviser, Brian Lentz, and Jeni gave me good guidance on that score. Frankly I disregarded the Met's advice. I felt they had never helped me constructively so far, so why should they be able to now? It was all just another nail in the coffin of my relationship with my former employers. I'd taken early retirement on medical grounds, not because I was old and crumbly and ready for a rest but because my heart knew, and my friends told me, that I had made the right decision for me as a person. But as Helen the WPC I had horrendous doubts, manifested in a series of distressing panic attacks triggered by just the thought of it. These were the ripples from the storm I had lived through. And they were seemingly endless.

That April I was to have attended an awards ceremony to receive an Assistant Commissioner's Commendation for my part in the lead up to shooting. But as I'd gone into labour and given birth to our daughter, Molly, two days before the ceremony, it was rescheduled for July. I duly attended Chigwell Police Club that summer with Steve, Ben and Molly. Nick Tinning was there too. And CJ came as my guest of honour. But, as usual, all was not as it seemed. There was a worm in the rose.

After the shooting the chief superintendent for Enfield, Dr Robert Wareing, had compiled a report recommending several of us involved in the incident for a Commissioner's Commendation. We were informed, and I was pleased to be considered for such an honour. As far as I knew it was all going through smoothly. I should have never assumed anything of the sort, because by doing so I set myself up to be knocked down. One day out of the blue I heard that a civilian employee at New Scotland Yard had decided in his infinite wisdom that as we were only doing what we had been trained to do, our award was to be downgraded. I thought this insensitive, to say the least, and lacking in logic. If it was so that we had only been doing our job, then surely that could be said about all the actions of every police officer. We could all be dismissed like that. I decided to let it go and resigned myself to the fact that what really mattered was that those of us who had been there that Boxing Day knew the score. And no pen-pusher from NSY could take that away from us.

I had one more go to see if I could hack police work, albeit this time as a civilian. In retrospect I think this was ill judged, given the residual memories of my earlier traumas, which might more easily be triggered by being back in a police environment.

On 13 October 1997 I went to work at Enfield station in the Divisional Intelligence Unit to take up my new role as a civilian administrative assistant. I badly missed my life as a police officer and wanted desperately to be back in the cut-and-thrust, even though I couldn't stand to watch violence on the TV or at the cinema any more, even though I had grown to hate crowds and had a special loathing for guns, even though I was a very different person from the fresh-faced country girl who wanted to help people and had joined the Met to do so. Part of me still yearned for it all — as it still does. I remember reading about WPC Harrison, when she was awarded the Queen's Commendation for Brave Conduct in 1994. She was reported in an article in the *Police Review* as saying that when she heard she could not return to work as a result of the attack that had almost killed her she was devastated and had no idea what the future held. She had been offered a desk job, but: 'To be that close to everybody and seeing them all going out on the street and knowing I had to stay chained to the office would be too much to bear.'

I could relate to that. I had only been at Enfield for two weeks and already I knew I'd made a mistake. The office-based work was no substitute for the beat of the street, and in many ways only made it harder for me to accept what I had lost. I was prepared to give it a go for a bit longer, but then something happened that changed my mind. One afternoon, just after lunch, as it often did, the phone rang. I answered it, expecting a query about some crime figures that had been released earlier in the week, but finding instead a newspaper journalist. What, she wanted to know, was my reaction to the death of Nina Mackay, the WPC who had just been stabbed to death while on duty in east London? I talked to her because I was too shocked to do otherwise. She asked me about the use of body armour and a mishmash of other details that I forget now.

Immediately the call ended, I went straight to the office of Chief Inspector Malcolm Wandrag. I felt totally stunned.

I could not understand how I had been found. I thought I was working somewhere safe, but the journalist, apparently working for the *Daily Mirror*, had reached me on my direct line. Who had handed out my number to her? No one knew I was there, because no one needed to. But the press were hounding me again, they'd got my scent, and this time I'd gone to earth. I walked out that day and never went back.

On my behalf, Steve complained to the commissioner's staff officer, but all he could manage was, 'Sorry, mate, I don't know how it happened.' Steve made a few further inquiries, but it got him nowhere. He was angry by now for all sorts of reasons, but most especially because I was off sick again. I wasn't exactly back where I'd started but I'd been certified sick with stress by my GP.

The Met took up the cudgels on my behalf. In January 1998 Dr Robert Wareing, divisional commander of Enfield Division, wrote to Piers Morgan, the editor of the *Daily Mirror*, to express, as he put it, 'my concern at the actions of one of your reporters, Amanda Ward, and the devastating effect it has had on a member of my staff'. He said, quite rightly, that I had had no reason to expect the call and described its effect on me as devastating. 'It rekindled,' he wrote, 'all kinds of negative emotions assorted with her trauma and caused her enormous stress. Since receiving that call Helen has been placed sick and her full recovery has been put back months by that one telephone call. This has not only affected her, but also her family, who are very upset by what has happened.'

Robert Wareing went on to remind Mr Morgan that the Met had co-operated fully with the media over the death of WPC Mackay, and that approaching me about it had been unnecessary and taking things to the extreme. He also suggested that in future some thought should be given by the press to the effect that events like this have on people, and that any such approaches should be made more appropriately by them through the Met's press office.

Piers Morgan's reply arrived a week later. He was, he wrote, very concerned about the disturbing effect his reporter's phone call had had on me and offered an assurance that no malice had been intended. With the benefit of hindsight he conceded that, in the circumstances, it had been insensitive of them to make direct contact with me. He had taken steps, he said, to ensure that in the future they did not make such approaches to people in my position. There was an apology, too, but as far as I was concerned it came too late because the damage had been done. The following month my solicitors, Russell Jones & Walker, sent me back once more to see Gordon Turnbull. He diagnosed that I had been retraumatised by the experience, and that I needed further treatment.

In the summer of 1998 I was interviewed by consultant psychiatrist Dr Duncan Veasey, again on the instruction of my solicitors. He'd been requested to ascertain whether, in his view, I had suffered from any psychiatric disorder as a result of trauma suffered during my police service. The night before I went to see him I had a nightmare, triggered by a shooting on the television news. Just like ours on Boxing Day 1994, it involved a helicopter landing, an ambulance and bodies. Steve told me that I was more restless than usual that night. I even hit out at him in my sleep, which I tend to do now.

When I was sent a copy of the report in August 1998, Dr Veasey had concluded that, prior to 1991, I appeared to have coped perfectly well with police work. He assessed me as suffering from PTSD of moderate to severe degree, which had become chronic, until the shooting when my symptoms had increased to be present to a severe degree. In terms of causation he believes that this condition first developed after the stabbing incident in 1991, that the IRA bombings markedly exacerbated my symptoms, that the shooting sent it off the map, and that in the balance of probabilities I am likely to be chronically psychiatrically disabled. His opinion was that there was little point in considering further treatment until the litigation process was completed as this was always a perpetuating factor, surrounded as it is by all sorts of resentments and stress. He believed that I had been seriously affected by the fact that I thought I had been deprived of treatment, which had been given to one of my colleagues — Jeni Lawson — simply because of cost. Given the potential for serious adverse publicity, he found it hard to understand why the Met didn't appear to want to settle my case promptly.

And so it goes on. I still have flashbacks and dreams. Sometimes these depict the actual events, sometimes they move on to related themes of danger and death. I still make a huge effort to avoid the memories. I distract myself by using the gym and avoid any connection with the police or talking about them. I have become progressively less interested in activities that I used to enjoy, such as socialising. Most of the time I feel detached, estranged from other people, and emotionally numb. This is not good for any of my relationships. I still don't sleep well. I am easily irritated and prone to sudden outbursts of anger. Concentration is not easy. Nor is dealing with the sense of being at risk, even when there is no obvious reason to be so. Nor do I find it easy to live with the startle reactions to loud, unexpected noises or movements that occur once or twice a week, and the heavy sweating and thudding of my heart that happens when I have a flashback. The Criminal Injuries Compensation Board (CICB) have still not yet settled with me. The most recent development is that I have now to go for a Magnetic Resonance Imaging (MRI) scan on my knee. God knows when I shall be finished with it. I only know I shall be glad when that day dawns.

I am a great believer in fate, and I know that things happen for a reason, even if that seems hard to understand at the time. I know that the bad things in life have their purpose as much as the good, and at the end of the day I am lucky to be alive and to be able to see the sun rise and set. I am different now. Life affects me more. I have a loving husband, two beautiful children. I am living my life accordingly. I have changed. What I would like to think is that the Met might change, too, so that it doesn't put its serving officers through the torment that I have endured — and still endure.

When I first left the job I felt as if I had lost my identity. Every time I saw a patrol car drive by I felt an aching sense of loss. But this has lessened as time's gone by, and the message I have is clear. I am not in the life-or-death business any more. I am for life. And life agrees with me. I now try to surround myself with people I like and things I like. I hear the birds sing, I notice the seasons and smell the flowers. What a wonderful world! Was it all here before?

Through some very difficult times my husband Steve has been very kind and supportive. He and I moved in together in late October 1996. In him I have found a wonderful man. Our baby Molly was born in April 1997, and in the

September we got married — yes, in that order! — in picturesque Broadway, Worcestershire. Ben was our pageboy, looking smart in his grey waistcoat and bow-tie and a pair of very grown-up pinstripe trousers. He loves his new dad, and his new sister, and on the surface at least he appears to be a happy, well-adjusted little boy. A year later, despite my troublesome knee, I ran a half-marathon and shortly after that qualified as a reflexologist. In early 1999 I found out that I was pregnant again. That spring we moved back to Worcestershire to try finally to lay old ghosts to rest and start again. I have come full circle. But you never can step into the same river twice.